TABLE OF CONTENTS

PREFACE TO THE THIRD EDITION OF THE GUIDE

This Guide is intended to help a data analyst select from the vast array of statistical techniques a statistic or technique that can be appropriately applied in a particular analysis. The Guide is addressed to social scientists, data analysts, and graduate students who have some knowledge of social science statistics and who want a systematic, highly condensed overview of current statistical techniques and their uses. It is not intended as a substitute for expert statistical consultation; if not already available, such expertise should always be sought prior to conducting a study.

The popularity of the first and second editions of this Guide, published under the title *A Guide for Selecting Statistical Techniques for Analyzing Social Science Data*, leads us to hope that this updated third edition will also prove useful. The original version of the Guide became available in 1971, was revised and formally published by the University of Michigan's Institute for Social Research in 1974, and subsequently went through four printings. The Guide has been translated and printed in Chinese, French, Gujarati, Hebrew, and Spanish. It has also been implemented in several computer applications.

This third edition contains most of the statistics and techniques that appeared in the first two editions, with additions and revisions to incorporate recent statistical and analytical developments.

No guide could (or should) include all the statistics ever proposed as useful for social science data analysis, and this Guide makes no claim to do so. Rather, it attempts to include, and functionally distinguish, those statistics and statistical techniques that are in common use in the social sciences, that receive significant attention in social science statistics texts, or that seem to have potential usefulness. About 160 statistics or techniques are included in this Guide.

The Guide begins with a short set of instructions about how to use the Guide and some alternative strategies and certain cautions that should be kept in mind. The core of the Guide consists of two parts. The first part is a 32-page "decision tree," a series of sequential questions and answers that lead the user to an appropriate statistic or statistical technique. Following the "tree" is a part on implementation, which describes the specific SAS procedures or techniques to use to obtain the particular statistic or technique. The SAS implementation is keyed to the decision tree pages. For example, information on implementation of a statistic on page 5 of the tree will be found under "page 5" in the implementation part. Appendix A, which is also keyed to the decision tree, provides sources of information about each statistic presented in the Guide. Appendix B notes some additional statistical techniques not covered in the Guide for various reasons. The Guide concludes with three additional sections: a glossary, which defines selected terms used in the decision tree; a bibliography that presents the full reference for each cited book, chapter, or article; and an alphabetical index of statistics and techniques.

This third edition of the Guide owes much to the contributions and leadership of Frank M. Andrews (1935-1992) in producing the first two editions. In the summer of 1992, four of the present authors (Andrews, Klem, O'Malley, and Rodgers) met to discuss the possibility of a third edition. Frank was very pleased at the success of the first two editions of our modest Guide, and was eager to produce a third edition. Indeed, Frank prepared the first draft of the preface to the third edition. Sadly, Frank passed away in December 1992, at the age of 57.

This third edition, unlike the first two, is being published by SAS Institute Inc. We appreciate the assistance and guidance during preparation provided by Julie Platt of the SAS User Publishing Program and Jennifer Ginn. Preparation was supported in part by SAS Institute and in part by a grant from the University of Michigan to Laura Klem. For assistance in the preparation of this Guide we are grateful to Patricia Bradley.

INSTRUCTIONS AND COMMENTS ON THE USE OF THE GUIDE

The Guide is intended to help a data analyst select statistics or statistical techniques appropriate for the purposes and conditions of a particular analysis.

To use the Guide, start with the questions on page 3, choose one of the answers presented there, and then continue along the "branches" of the decision tree as instructed. Eventually you will arrive at a box that names a statistical technique or a statistical measure or a statistical test appropriate to your situation, if one was known to the authors. Many of the technical terms used in the Guide are defined in the Glossary.

The typical box contains one statistical measure (in the portion outlined by solid lines) and one statistical test (in the dotted portion). In a few cases, several different measures or several different tests are presented in the same box. These tests and measures are essentially equivalent from a functional point of view, and comments to help you choose among them may appear in an accompanying footnote. Sometimes a measure appears without an accompanying test if none seemed particularly appropriate; and sometimes a test is listed without any measure.

Some branches of the tree terminate in boxes for which the authors knew of no specific technique — indeed, further statistical development may be needed. If an analysis is to be performed in such a case, it will be necessary to find an alternative sequence through the decision tree or to consult with another source of information.

In many analysis situations, it is possible to make alternative decisions about the nature of the variables, relationships, and/or goals, and these may result in the selection of alternative final boxes. It is always possible to use techniques that require less stringent assumptions than the ones originally considered. For example, measures or tests may be used that are appropriate for a weaker scale of measurement; or techniques appropriate for non-additive situations may be used even though the variables actually form an additive system. Note also that non-additive systems can sometimes be handled using an additive technique if an appropriate combination of variables (for example, a product variable) has been formed. Recall also that ranks and two-point nominal variables meet the definition of intervally scaled variables.

Cautionary comments

1. Weighted data, missing data, small sample sizes, complex sample designs, and capitalization on chance in fitting a statistical model are sources of potential problems in data analysis. A frequent problem with survey data, in particular, is the lack of independence of the observations. That is, the probability of selection of one case for inclusion in the sample may be related to the probability of selection of other cases, which is a violation of an assumption underlying standard expressions for the estimation of variances and, thus, of confidence intervals and test statistics. The Guide does not deal with these complications. If one of these situations exists, the Guide

should be used with caution. See note 2 in Appendix B for a brief discussion of sampling errors from complex surveys.

2. The statistical measures in the terminal boxes are descriptive of the particular sample being examined. For some statistical measures, the value obtained will also be a good estimate of the value in the population as a whole, whereas other statistics may underestimate (or overestimate) the population value. In general, the amount of bias is relatively small and sometimes adjustments can be made for it. These adjustments are discussed in some statistics texts (but not in the Guide).

3. In principle, a confidence interval may be placed around any statistic. It is also possible to test the significance of the difference between values of a statistic calculated for two non-overlapping groups. These procedures are not indicated in the Guide but are discussed in standard textbooks.

4. The Guide does not explicitly consider possible transformations of the data such as bracketing, using logarithms, and ranking. Transformations may be used to simplify analysis or to bring data into line with assumptions. (For example, it is often possible to transform scores so that they correspond more closely to a normal distribution, constitute an interval scale, or relate linearly to another variable.) The Guide does point to the use of polynomial terms to take account of non-linear relationships, but it does not deal with other techniques that are sometimes useful for the same reason, such as piecewise regression. Occasionally, it may be wise to eliminate cases with extreme values. See Snedecor and Cochran (1989, page 282) for information on transformations.

5. To incorporate nominal (qualitative) variables as predictors in regression models, it is often useful to convert those variables into sets of indicator ("dummy") variables. This is also useful for dealing with ordinal variables, for dealing with interval variables that have non-linear relationships with the dependent variable, and for taking account of cases with missing values on otherwise intervally scaled variables.

6. In addition to the assumption of independence discussed in Comment 1, there are two additional common assumptions for inferences based on techniques using one or more intervally scaled variables (particularly when the intervally scaled variable is a dependent variable). The first assumption is that the observations are drawn from a population normally distributed on the intervally scaled variable(s). (This assumption is less critical as the sample size increases.) The second assumption is that, if more than one variable is involved, the intervally scaled variable(s) have equal variances within categories of the other variables. That is, there is homogeneity of variance. Bivariate or multivariate normality is also sometimes assumed.

7. For nominal and ordinal variables, it is necessary to assign numbers to the categories in order to implement some of the procedures described in the Guide.

THE DECISION TREE:
QUESTIONS AND ANSWERS LEADING TO APPROPRIATE STATISTICS OR STATISTICAL TECHNIQUES

<u>STARTING POINT</u>

How many variables does the problem involve?

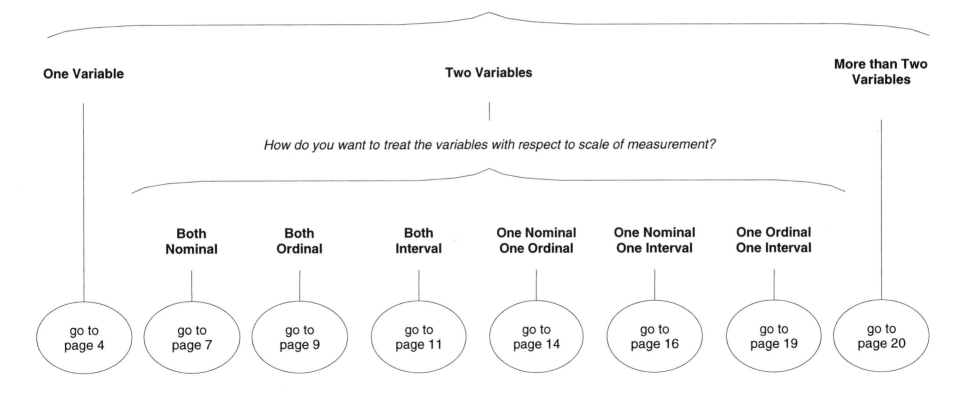

One Variable

Two Variables

More than Two Variables

How do you want to treat the variables with respect to scale of measurement?

| Both Nominal | Both Ordinal | Both Interval | One Nominal One Ordinal | One Nominal One Interval | One Ordinal One Interval |

go to page 4

go to page 7

go to page 9

go to page 11

go to page 14

go to page 16

go to page 19

go to page 20

ONE VARIABLE

How do you want to treat the variable with respect to scale of measurement?

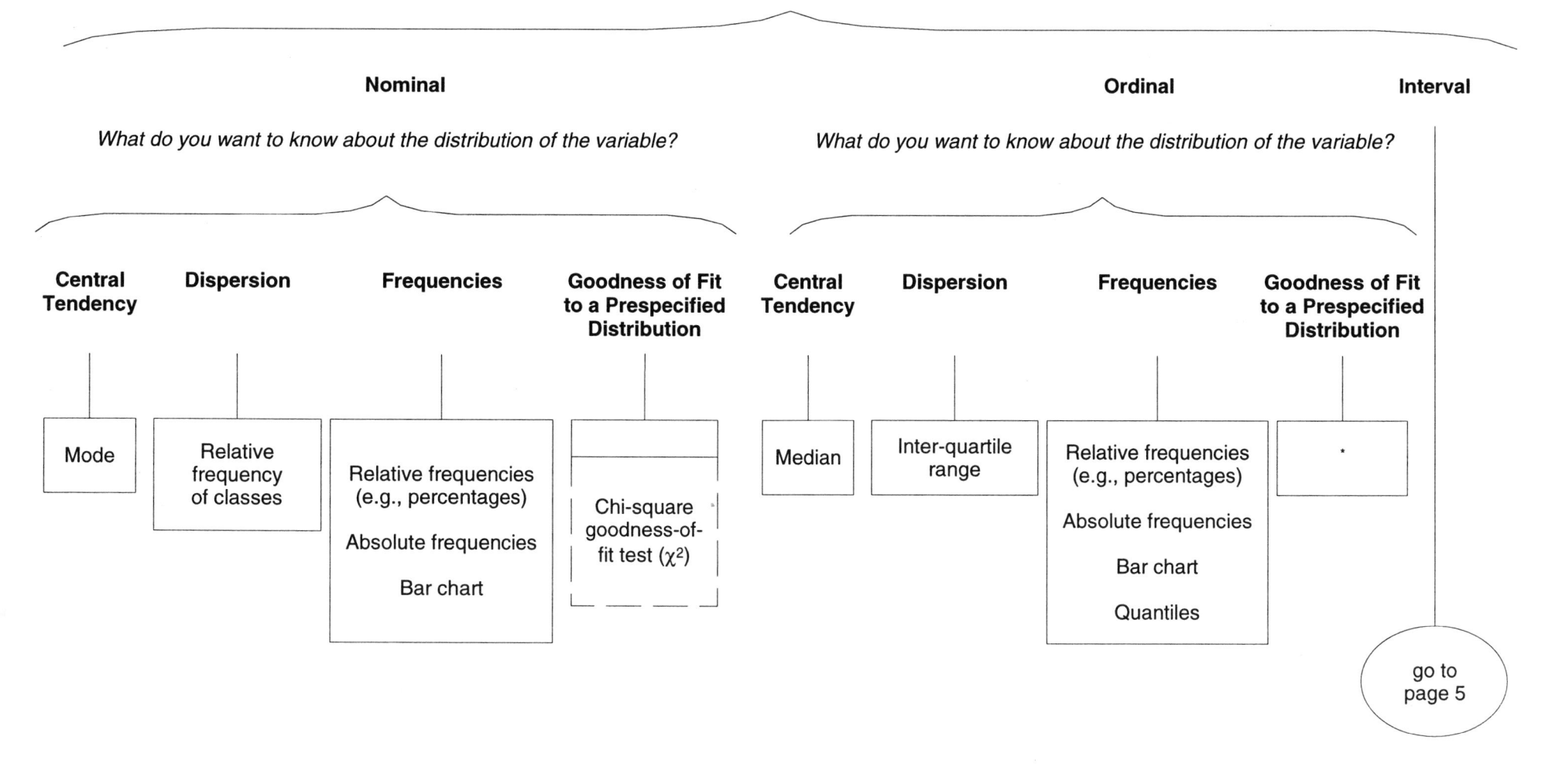

Nominal

Ordinal   **Interval**

What do you want to know about the distribution of the variable?   *What do you want to know about the distribution of the variable?*

Central Tendency	Dispersion	Frequencies	Goodness of Fit to a Prespecified Distribution	Central Tendency	Dispersion	Frequencies	Goodness of Fit to a Prespecified Distribution
Mode	Relative frequency of classes	Relative frequencies (e.g., percentages) Absolute frequencies Bar chart	Chi-square goodness-of-fit test (χ^2)	Median	Inter-quartile range	Relative frequencies (e.g., percentages) Absolute frequencies Bar chart Quantiles	*

go to page 5

*If you are willing to ignore the ordinal property of your variable, you can use the chi-square goodness-of-fit test for a nominal variable.

ONE VARIABLE: Interval (continued from page 4)

What do you want to know about the distribution of the variable?

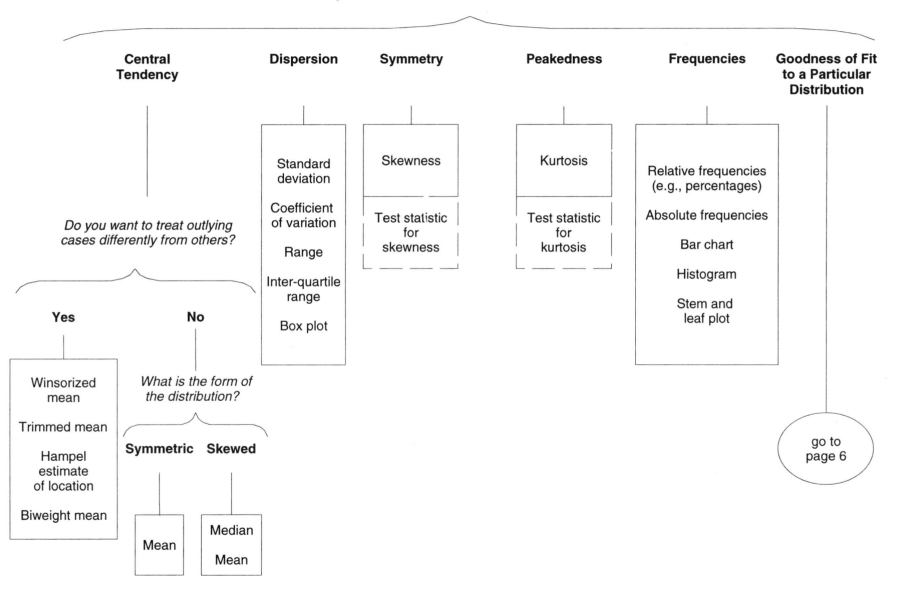

ONE VARIABLE: Interval (continued from page 5)

● You want to know the goodness of fit to a particular distribution

Do you want to treat the variable as continuous or discrete?

Continuous

Is the particular distribution normal?

Discrete

Is the particular distribution Poisson (that is, is the variable a count of events, and do you want to test if the events are independent with the same probability of occurrence)?

Yes (Normal)

Kolmogorov-Smirnov one sample test

Shapiro-Wilk test

Superimposition of normal density over histogram of your variable

Superimposition of cumulative normal distribution over cumulative distribution of your variable

Q-Q plot

See also specific tests for skewness and kurtosis

No (e.g., Weibull, Exponential, Log-Normal)

Kolmogorov-Smirnov one sample test

Superimposition of particular density over histogram of your variable

Superimposition of cumulative particular distribution over cumulative distribution of your variable

Q-Q plot

Yes

Kolmogorov-Smirnov one sample test

Chi-square goodness-of-fit test (χ^2)

No

*

*If you are willing to ignore the interval level properties of your variable, the goodness-of-fit test for a nominal variable may be appropriate. Or you may prefer to treat the variable as continuous.

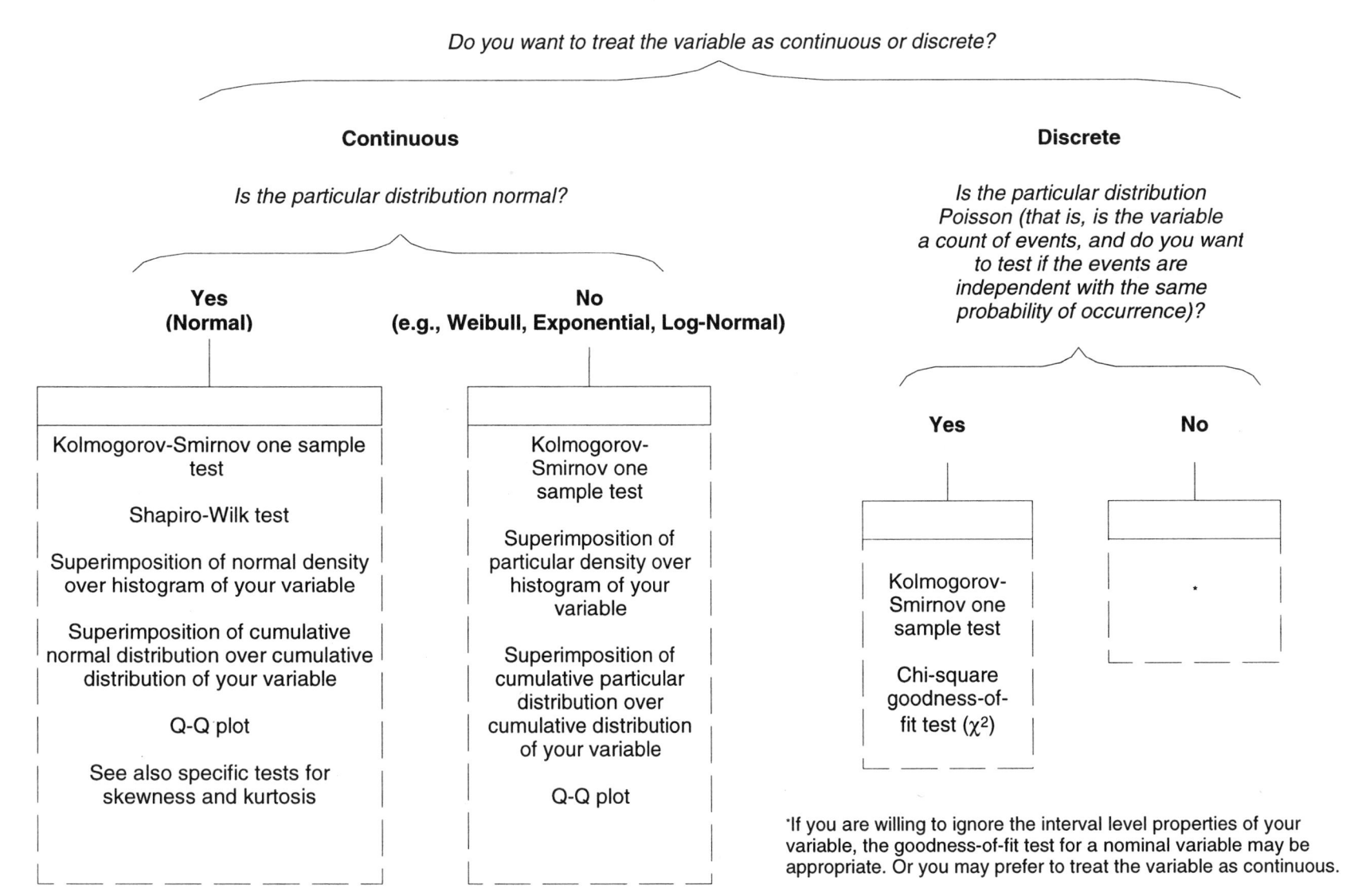

TWO VARIABLES: Both Nominal

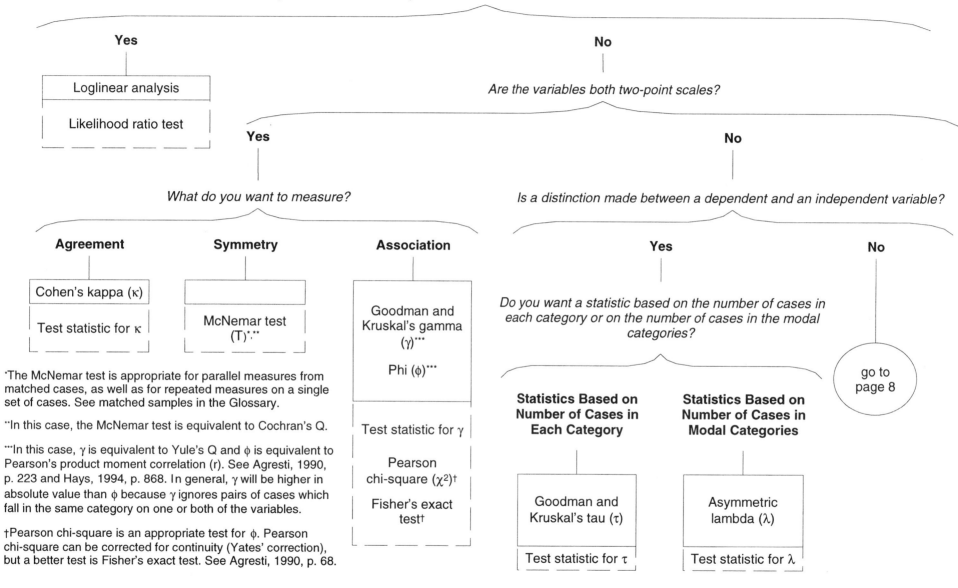

Do you want to model frequencies in the cross tabulation of the two variables?

Yes

Loglinear analysis

Likelihood ratio test

No

Are the variables both two-point scales?

Yes

What do you want to measure?

Agreement

Cohen's kappa (κ)

Test statistic for κ

Symmetry

McNemar test (T)*,**

Association

Goodman and Kruskal's gamma (γ)***

Phi (φ)***

Test statistic for γ

Pearson chi-square (χ²)†

Fisher's exact test†

*The McNemar test is appropriate for parallel measures from matched cases, as well as for repeated measures on a single set of cases. See matched samples in the Glossary.

**In this case, the McNemar test is equivalent to Cochran's Q.

***In this case, γ is equivalent to Yule's Q and φ is equivalent to Pearson's product moment correlation (r). See Agresti, 1990, p. 223 and Hays, 1994, p. 868. In general, γ will be higher in absolute value than φ because γ ignores pairs of cases which fall in the same category on one or both of the variables.

†Pearson chi-square is an appropriate test for φ. Pearson chi-square can be corrected for continuity (Yates' correction), but a better test is Fisher's exact test. See Agresti, 1990, p. 68.

No

Is a distinction made between a dependent and an independent variable?

Yes

Do you want a statistic based on the number of cases in each category or on the number of cases in the modal categories?

Statistics Based on Number of Cases in Each Category

Goodman and Kruskal's tau (τ)

Test statistic for τ

Statistics Based on Number of Cases in Modal Categories

Asymmetric lambda (λ)

Test statistic for λ

No

go to page 8

TWO VARIABLES: Both Nominal (continued from page 7)

● At least one of the variables is not a two-point scale ● No distinction is made between a dependent and an independent variable

What do you want to measure?

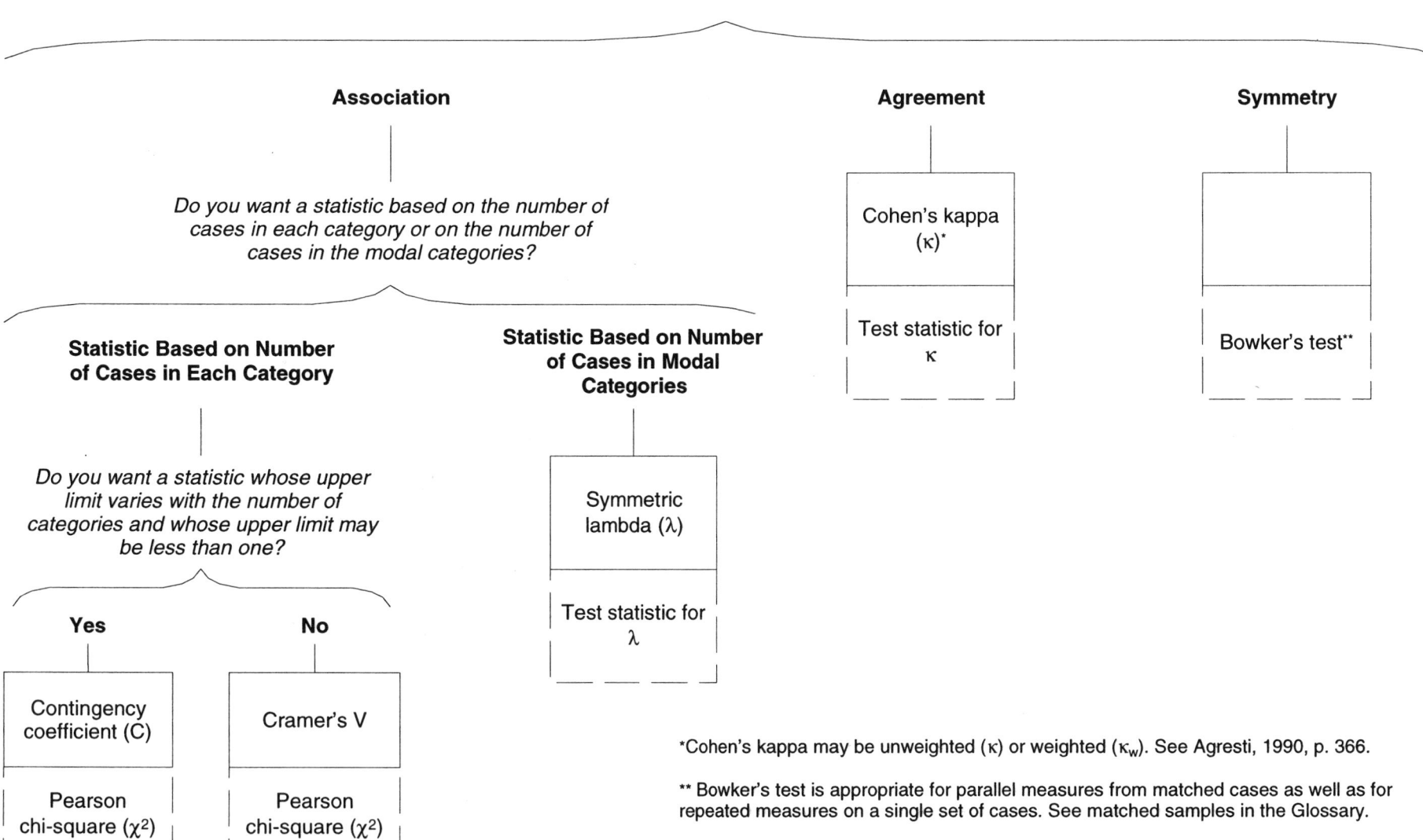

Association

Do you want a statistic based on the number of cases in each category or on the number of cases in the modal categories?

Statistic Based on Number of Cases in Each Category

Do you want a statistic whose upper limit varies with the number of categories and whose upper limit may be less than one?

Yes

Contingency coefficient (C)

Pearson chi-square (χ^2)

No

Cramer's V

Pearson chi-square (χ^2)

Statistic Based on Number of Cases in Modal Categories

Symmetric lambda (λ)

Test statistic for λ

Agreement

Cohen's kappa (κ)*

Test statistic for κ

Symmetry

Bowker's test**

*Cohen's kappa may be unweighted (κ) or weighted (κ_w). See Agresti, 1990, p. 366.

** Bowker's test is appropriate for parallel measures from matched cases as well as for repeated measures on a single set of cases. See matched samples in the Glossary.

TWO VARIABLES: Both Ordinal

Is a distinction made between dependent and independent variables?

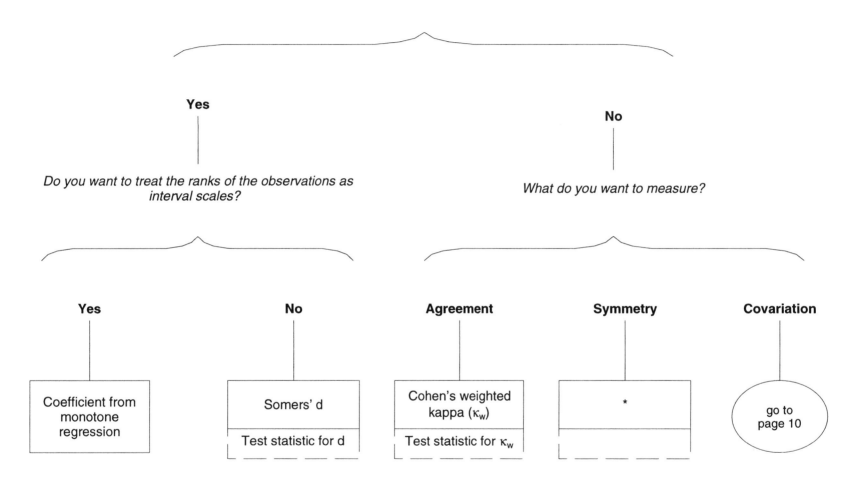

Yes

Do you want to treat the ranks of the observations as interval scales?

No

What do you want to measure?

Yes

Coefficient from monotone regression

No

Somers' d

Test statistic for d

Agreement

Cohen's weighted kappa (κ_w)

Test statistic for κ_w

Symmetry

*

Covariation

go to page 10

*For a discussion of symmetry models for ordinal data, see Agresti, 1990, p. 353.

TWO VARIABLES: Both Ordinal (continued from page 9)

● No distinction is made between dependent and independent variables ● You want to measure covariation

Do you want to treat the ranks of the observations as interval scales?

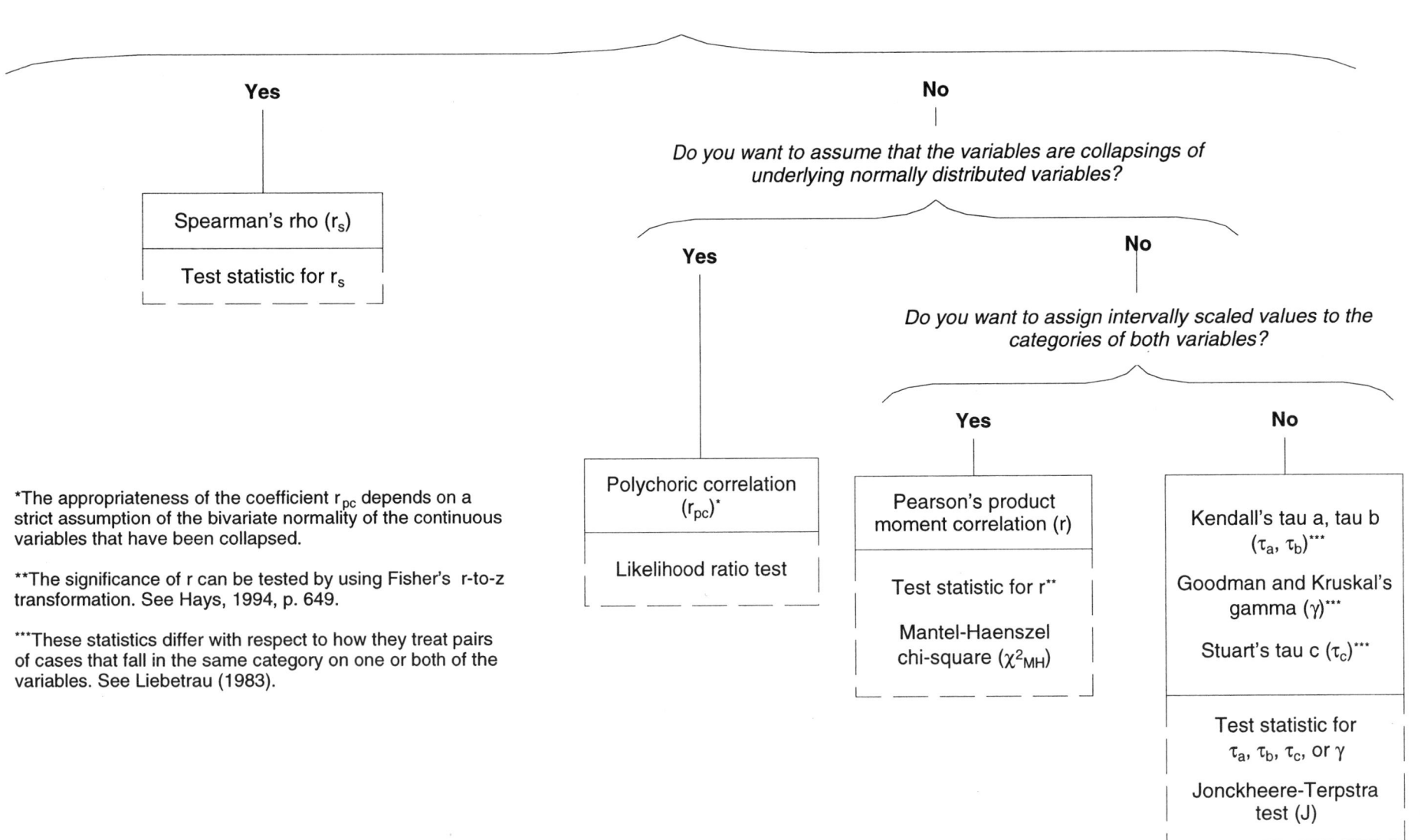

Yes

Spearman's rho (r_s)

Test statistic for r_s

No

Do you want to assume that the variables are collapsings of underlying normally distributed variables?

Yes

Polychoric correlation (r_{pc})*

Likelihood ratio test

No

Do you want to assign intervally scaled values to the categories of both variables?

Yes

Pearson's product moment correlation (r)

Test statistic for r**

Mantel-Haenszel chi-square (χ^2_{MH})

No

Kendall's tau a, tau b (τ_a, τ_b)***

Goodman and Kruskal's gamma (γ)***

Stuart's tau c (τ_c)***

Test statistic for τ_a, τ_b, τ_c, or γ

Jonckheere-Terpstra test (J)

*The appropriateness of the coefficient r_{pc} depends on a strict assumption of the bivariate normality of the continuous variables that have been collapsed.

**The significance of r can be tested by using Fisher's r-to-z transformation. See Hays, 1994, p. 649.

***These statistics differ with respect to how they treat pairs of cases that fall in the same category on one or both of the variables. See Liebetrau (1983).

TWO VARIABLES: Both Interval

Is a distinction made between a dependent and an independent variable?

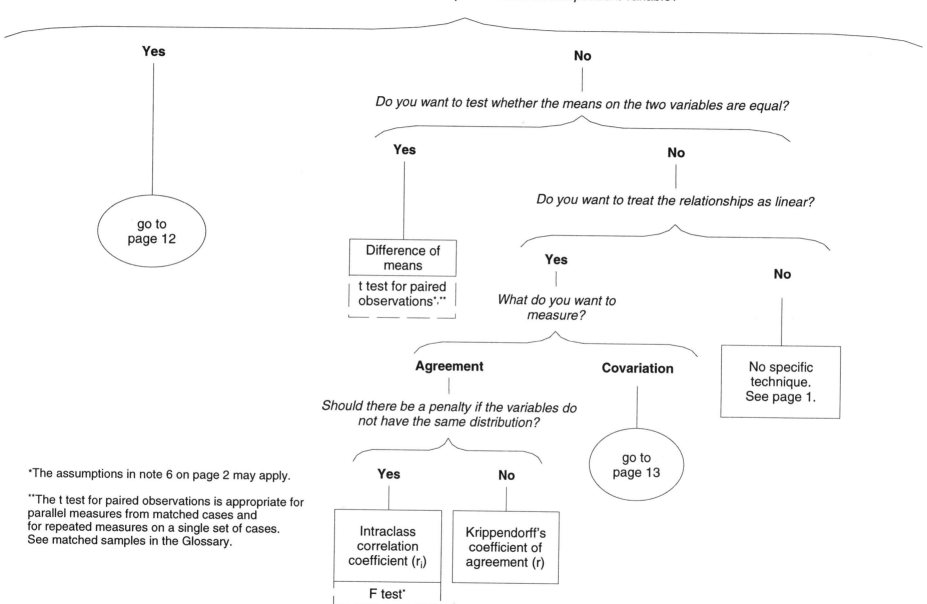

Yes

go to
page 12

No

Do you want to test whether the means on the two variables are equal?

Yes

Difference of
means

t test for paired
observations*,**

No

Do you want to treat the relationships as linear?

Yes

*What do you want to
measure?*

Agreement

*Should there be a penalty if the variables do
not have the same distribution?*

Yes

Intraclass
correlation
coefficient (r_i)

F test*

No

Krippendorff's
coefficient of
agreement (r)

Covariation

go to
page 13

No

No specific
technique.
See page 1.

*The assumptions in note 6 on page 2 may apply.

**The t test for paired observations is appropriate for
parallel measures from matched cases and
for repeated measures on a single set of cases.
See matched samples in the Glossary.

TWO VARIABLES: Both Interval (continued from page 11)

● A distinction is made between an independent and a dependent variable

Is the dependent variable dichotomous?

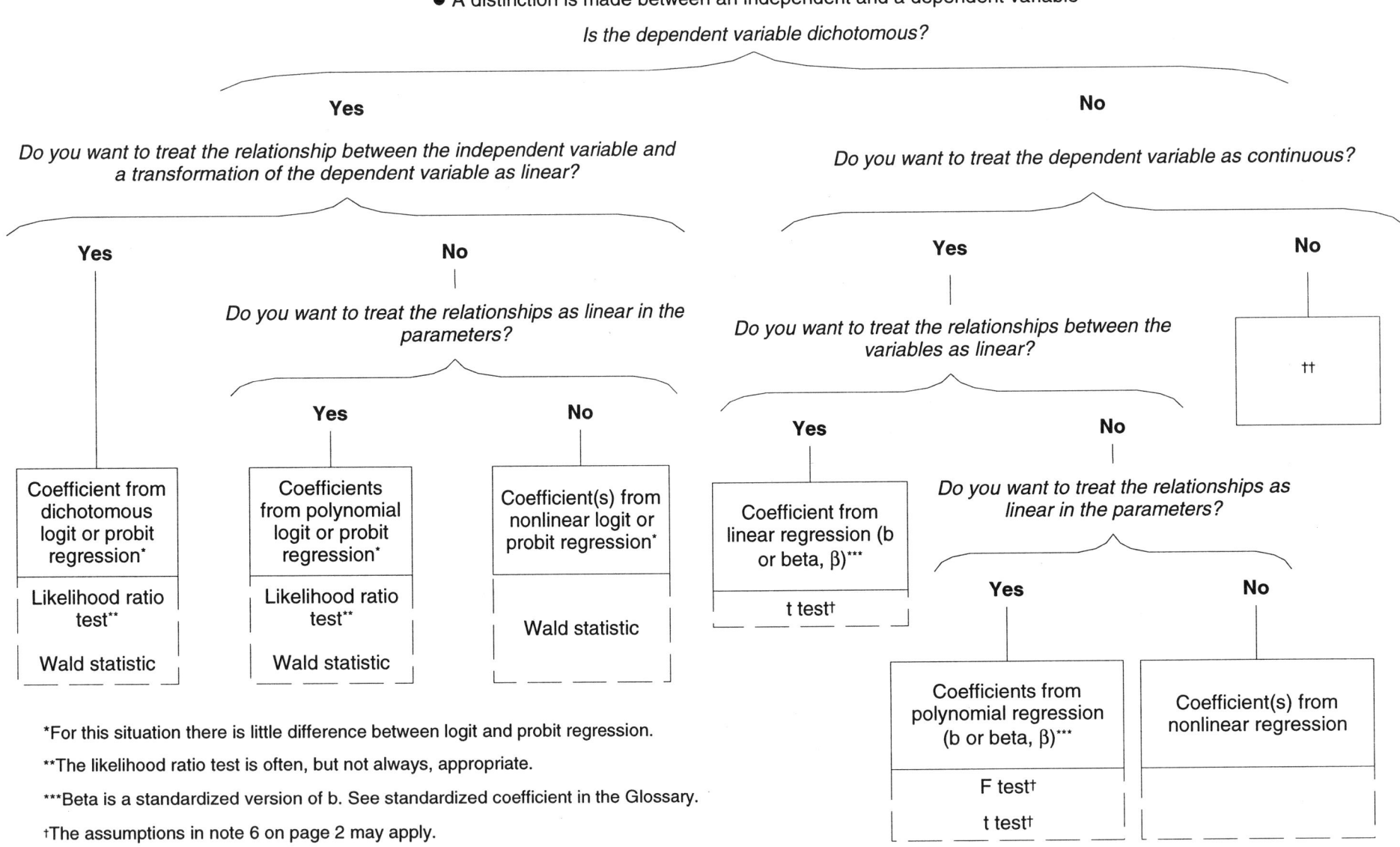

Yes

Do you want to treat the relationship between the independent variable and a transformation of the dependent variable as linear?

Yes

No

Do you want to treat the relationships as linear in the parameters?

Yes

No

Coefficient from dichotomous logit or probit regression*
Likelihood ratio test**
Wald statistic

Coefficients from polynomial logit or probit regression*
Likelihood ratio test**
Wald statistic

Coefficient(s) from nonlinear logit or probit regression*
Wald statistic

No

Do you want to treat the dependent variable as continuous?

Yes

No

Do you want to treat the relationships between the variables as linear?

Yes

No

Coefficient from linear regression (b or beta, β)***
t test†

Do you want to treat the relationships as linear in the parameters?

Yes

No

Coefficients from polynomial regression (b or beta, β)***
F test†
t test†

Coefficient(s) from nonlinear regression

††

*For this situation there is little difference between logit and probit regression.

**The likelihood ratio test is often, but not always, appropriate.

***Beta is a standardized version of b. See standardized coefficient in the Glossary.

†The assumptions in note 6 on page 2 may apply.

††For a discussion of techniques for handling dependent variables that are counts, or limited in some other way, see Maddala (1983).

TWO VARIABLES: Both Interval (continued from page 11)

- ● No distinction is made between dependent and independent variable
- ● The relationship is to be treated as linear ● Covariation is to be measured

How many of the variables are dichotomous?

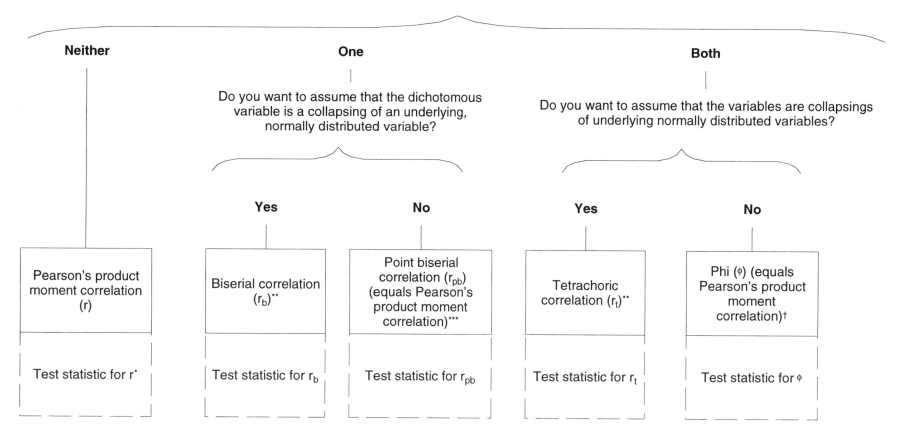

Neither

One

Do you want to assume that the dichotomous variable is a collapsing of an underlying, normally distributed variable?

Both

Do you want to assume that the variables are collapsings of underlying normally distributed variables?

Yes **No** **Yes** **No**

Pearson's product moment correlation (r)	Biserial correlation (r_b)**	Point biserial correlation (r_{pb}) (equals Pearson's product moment correlation)***	Tetrachoric correlation (r_t)**	Phi (ϕ) (equals Pearson's product moment correlation)†
Test statistic for r*	Test statistic for r_b	Test statistic for r_{pb}	Test statistic for r_t	Test statistic for ϕ

*The significance of r can be tested by using Fisher's r-to-z transformation. See Hays, 1994, p. 649.
**Both the r_b and the r_t depend on a strict assumption of the bivariate normality of the continuous variables that have been dichotomized.
***In this case, r_{pb} is mathematically equivalent to r; the tests are almost equivalent.
†In this case, ϕ is mathematically equivalent to r; the tests are almost equivalent.

TWO VARIABLES: One Nominal, One Ordinal

Is a distinction made between a dependent and an independent variable?

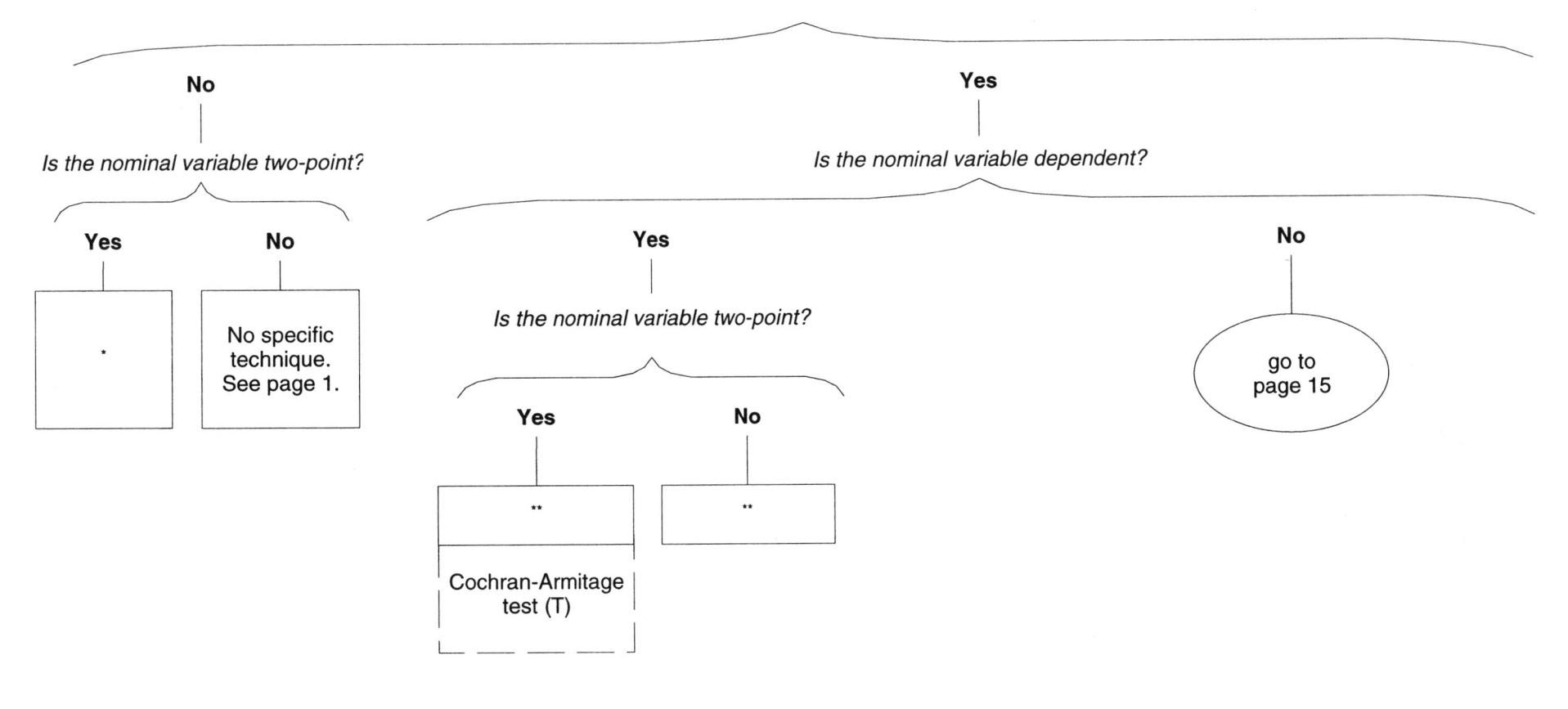

*You may wish to treat the ordinal variable as interval. For example, you could assign scores to the categories of the ordinal variable.

**Any two-point variable meets the criteria for both an ordinally and intervally scaled variable.

TWO VARIABLES: One Nominal, One Ordinal (continued from page 14)

● A distinction made between a dependent and an independent variable ● The nominal variable is independent

Are the cases (e.g., people) in one category of the nominal variable matched to the cases in the other category of that variable? *

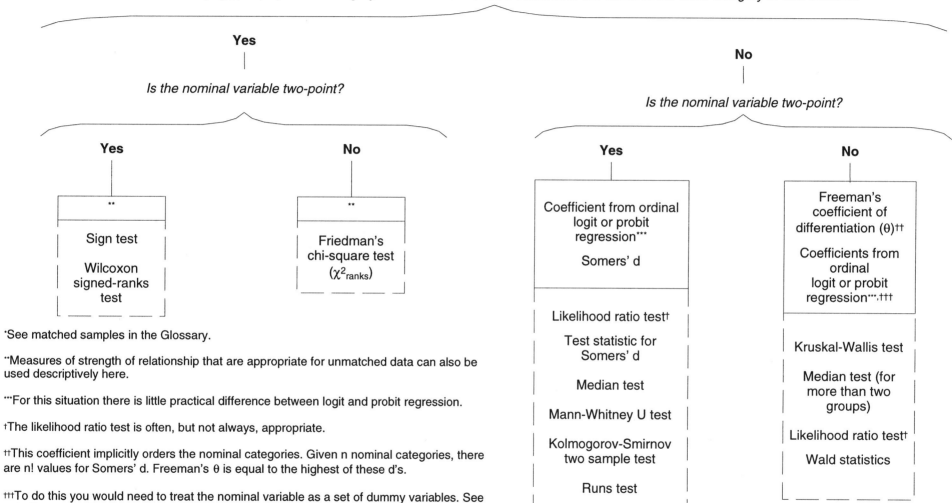

Yes

Is the nominal variable two-point?

Yes

**
Sign test

Wilcoxon
signed-ranks
test

No

**
Friedman's
chi-square test
(χ^2_{ranks})

No

Is the nominal variable two-point?

Yes

Coefficient from ordinal
logit or probit
regression***

Somers' d

Likelihood ratio test†

Test statistic for
Somers' d

Median test

Mann-Whitney U test

Kolmogorov-Smirnov
two sample test

Runs test

No

Freeman's
coefficient of
differentiation (θ)††

Coefficients from
ordinal
logit or probit
regression***,†††

Kruskal-Wallis test

Median test (for
more than two
groups)

Likelihood ratio test†

Wald statistics

·See matched samples in the Glossary.

··Measures of strength of relationship that are appropriate for unmatched data can also be used descriptively here.

···For this situation there is little practical difference between logit and probit regression.

†The likelihood ratio test is often, but not always, appropriate.

††This coefficient implicitly orders the nominal categories. Given n nominal categories, there are n! values for Somers' d. Freeman's θ is equal to the highest of these d's.

†††To do this you would need to treat the nominal variable as a set of dummy variables. See note 5 on page 2.

TWO VARIABLES: One Nominal, One Interval

Do you want to do survival analysis, i.e., do you want to analyze the nominal variable as a function of time, allowing for censored data?

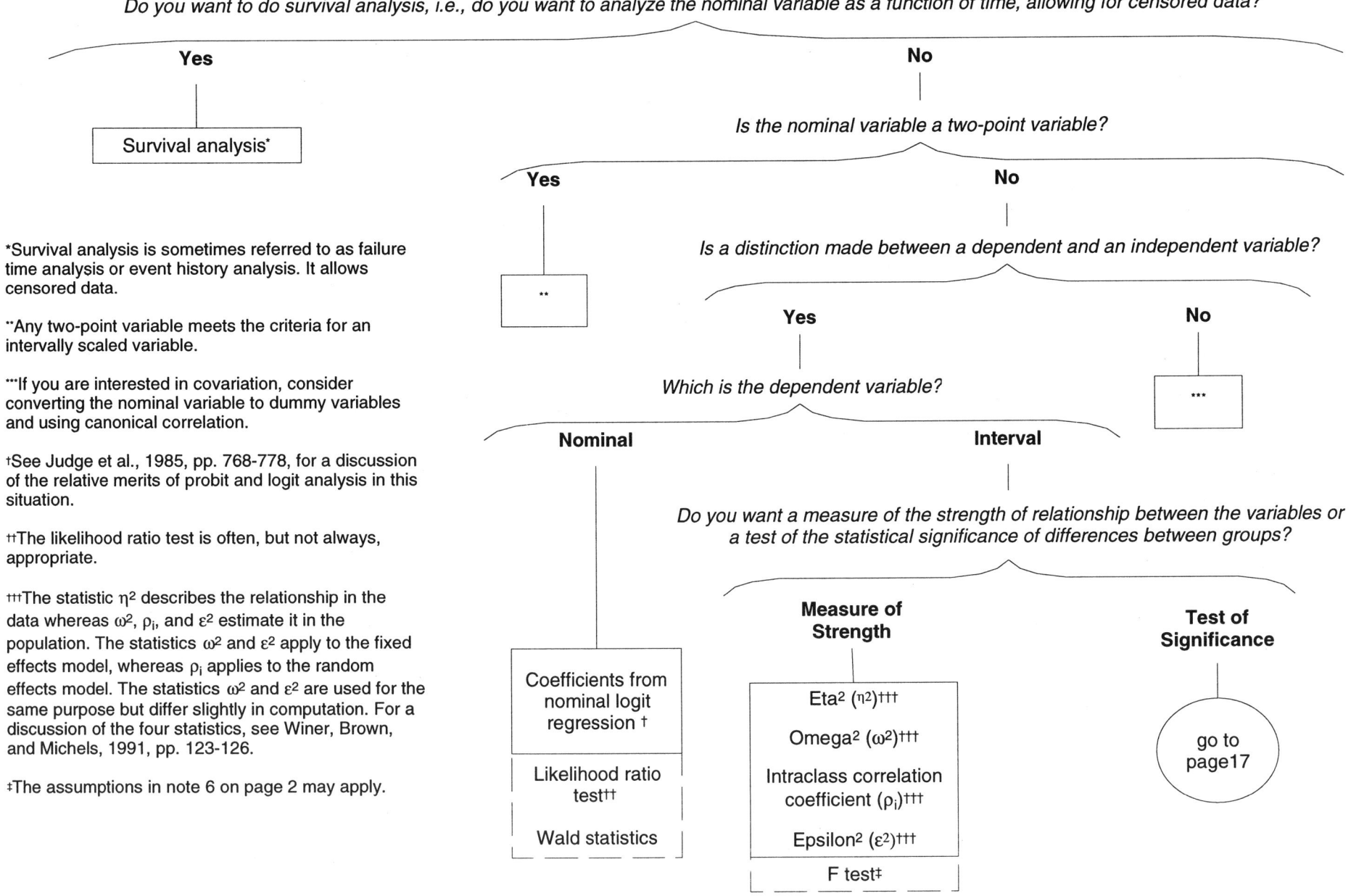

Yes

Survival analysis*

No

Is the nominal variable a two-point variable?

Yes

**

No

Is a distinction made between a dependent and an independent variable?

Yes

Which is the dependent variable?

No

***

Nominal

Coefficients from nominal logit regression †

Likelihood ratio test††

Wald statistics

Interval

Do you want a measure of the strength of relationship between the variables or a test of the statistical significance of differences between groups?

Measure of Strength

Eta² (η^2)†††

Omega² (ω^2)†††

Intraclass correlation coefficient (ρ_i)†††

Epsilon² (ε^2)†††

F test‡

Test of Significance

go to page17

*Survival analysis is sometimes referred to as failure time analysis or event history analysis. It allows censored data.

**Any two-point variable meets the criteria for an intervally scaled variable.

***If you are interested in covariation, consider converting the nominal variable to dummy variables and using canonical correlation.

†See Judge et al., 1985, pp. 768-778, for a discussion of the relative merits of probit and logit analysis in this situation.

††The likelihood ratio test is often, but not always, appropriate.

†††The statistic η^2 describes the relationship in the data whereas ω^2, ρ_i, and ε^2 estimate it in the population. The statistics ω^2 and ε^2 apply to the fixed effects model, whereas ρ_i applies to the random effects model. The statistics ω^2 and ε^2 are used for the same purpose but differ slightly in computation. For a discussion of the four statistics, see Winer, Brown, and Michels, 1991, pp. 123-126.

‡The assumptions in note 6 on page 2 may apply.

TWO VARIABLES: One Nominal, One Interval (continued from page 16)

● There are two variables, one interval and the other nominal ● The interval variable is dependent
● Statistical significance of differences between groups is to be tested

Are you willing to assume that the intervally scaled variable is normally distributed in the population?

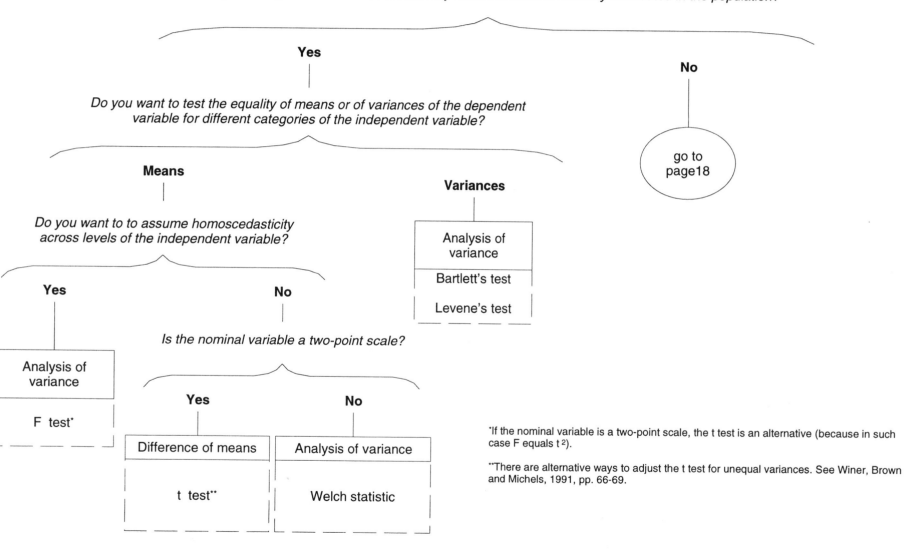

*If the nominal variable is a two-point scale, the t test is an alternative (because in such case F equals t^2).

**There are alternative ways to adjust the t test for unequal variances. See Winer, Brown and Michels, 1991, pp. 66-69.

TWO VARIABLES: One Nominal, One Interval (continued from page 17)

● There are two variables, one interval and the other nominal ● The interval variable is dependent ● Statistical significance of differences between groups is to be tested ● The interval variable is not assumed to be normally distributed in the population

Do you want to test the equality of variances of the dependent variable for different categories of the independent variable?

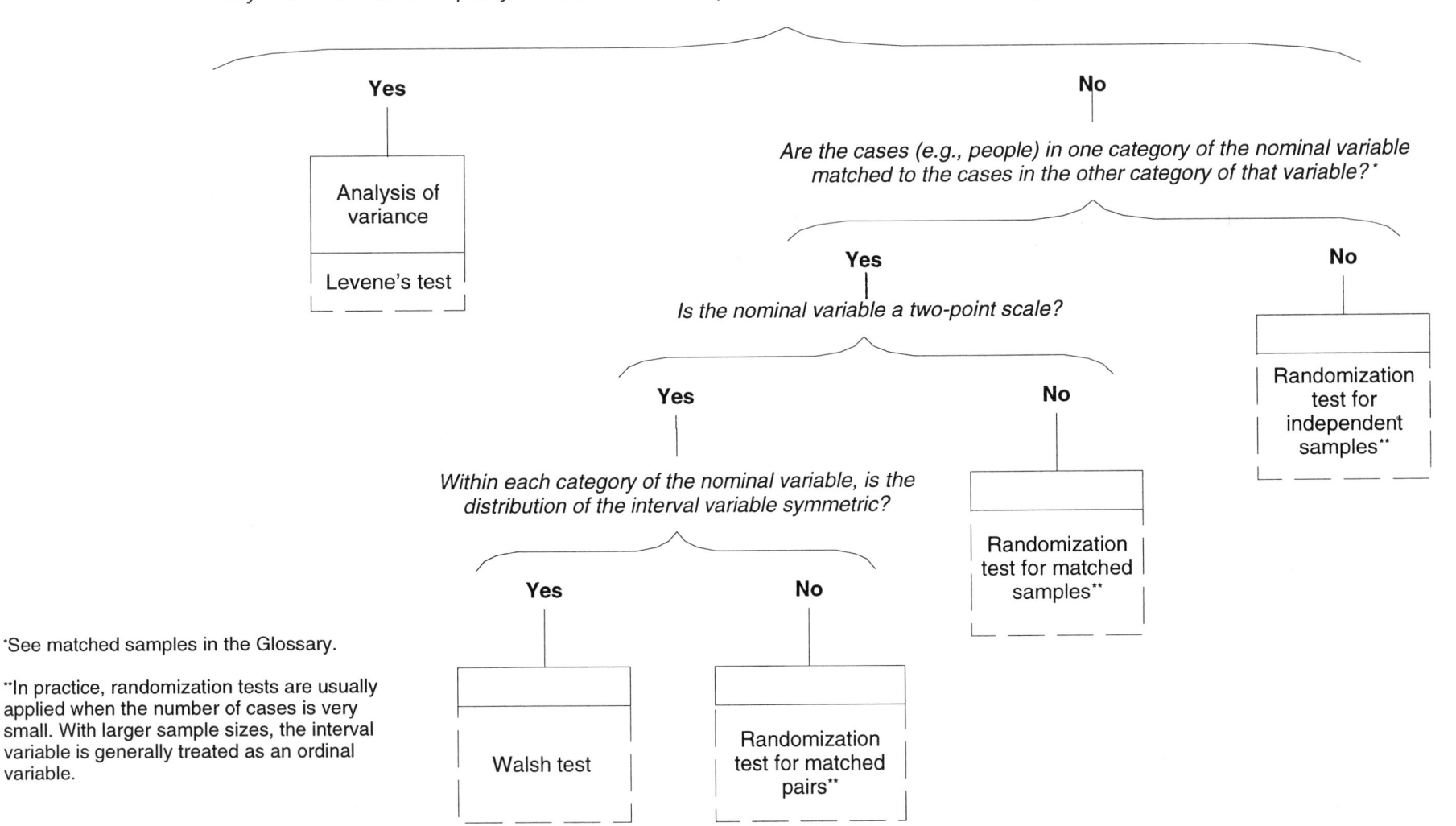

Yes

Analysis of variance

Levene's test

No

Are the cases (e.g., people) in one category of the nominal variable matched to the cases in the other category of that variable? *

Yes

Is the nominal variable a two-point scale?

Yes

Within each category of the nominal variable, is the distribution of the interval variable symmetric?

Yes

Walsh test

No

Randomization test for matched pairs**

No

Randomization test for matched samples**

No

Randomization test for independent samples**

*See matched samples in the Glossary.

**In practice, randomization tests are usually applied when the number of cases is very small. With larger sample sizes, the interval variable is generally treated as an ordinal variable.

TWO VARIABLES: One Ordinal, One Interval

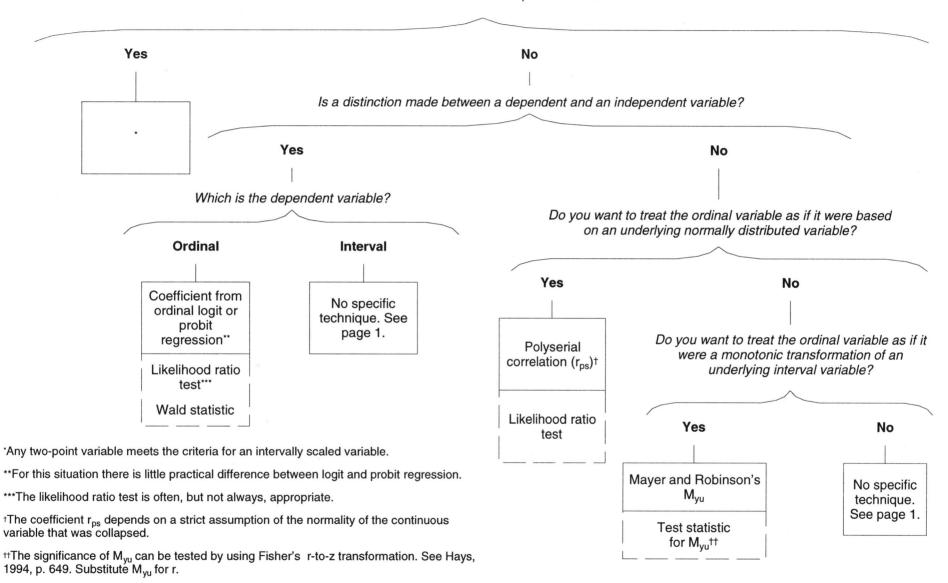

Is the ordinal variable a two-point variable?

Yes

*

No

Is a distinction made between a dependent and an independent variable?

Yes

Which is the dependent variable?

Ordinal

Coefficient from ordinal logit or probit regression**

Likelihood ratio test***

Wald statistic

Interval

No specific technique. See page 1.

No

Do you want to treat the ordinal variable as if it were based on an underlying normally distributed variable?

Yes

Polyserial correlation (r_{ps})†

Likelihood ratio test

No

Do you want to treat the ordinal variable as if it were a monotonic transformation of an underlying interval variable?

Yes

Mayer and Robinson's M_{yu}

Test statistic for M_{yu}††

No

No specific technique. See page 1.

*Any two-point variable meets the criteria for an intervally scaled variable.

**For this situation there is little practical difference between logit and probit regression.

***The likelihood ratio test is often, but not always, appropriate.

†The coefficient r_{ps} depends on a strict assumption of the normality of the continuous variable that was collapsed.

††The significance of M_{yu} can be tested by using Fisher's r-to-z transformation. See Hays, 1994, p. 649. Substitute M_{yu} for r.

MORE THAN TWO VARIABLES

Do you have the variables measured at more than one level, and do you want to model the relationship within and between levels?

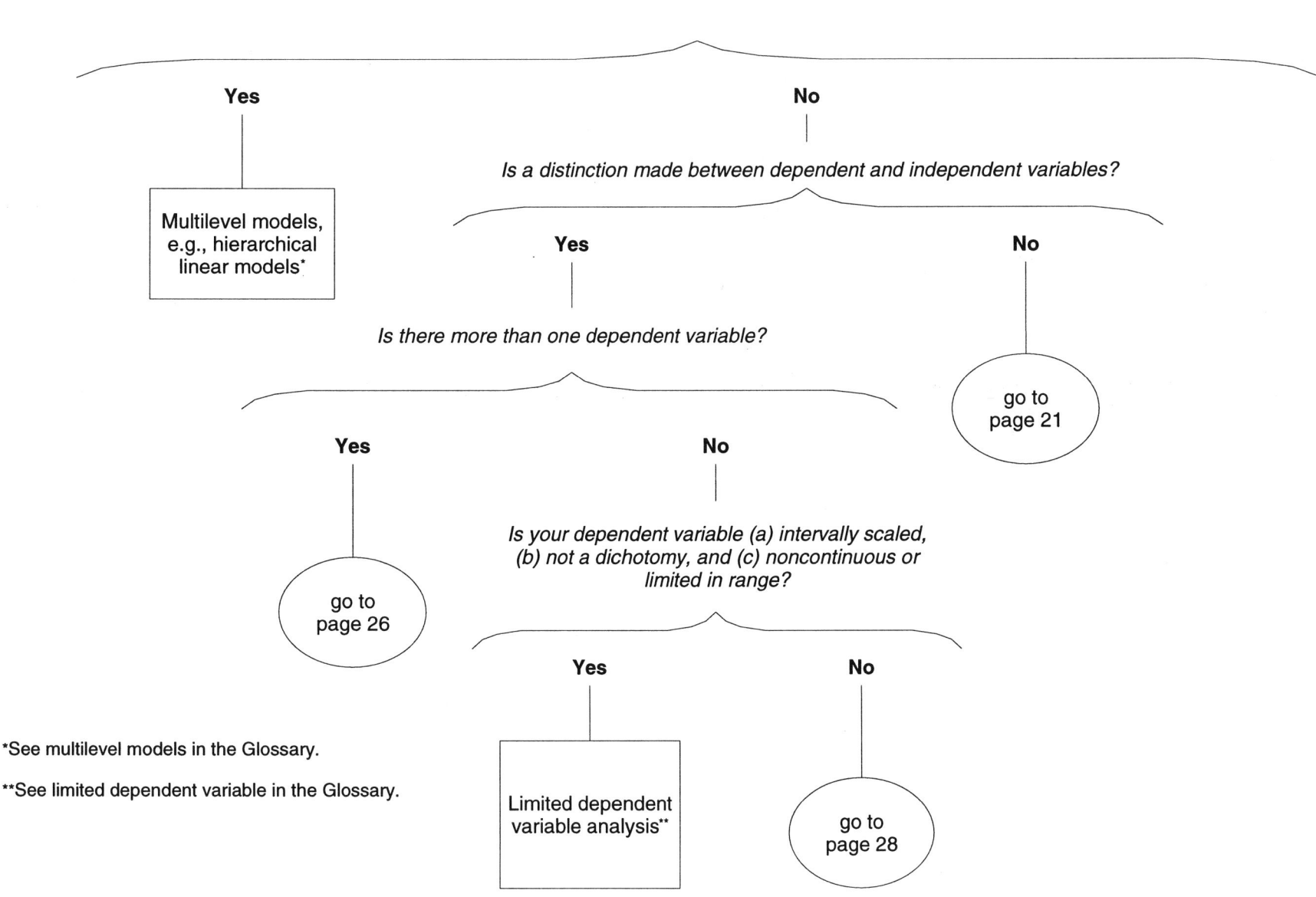

Yes

Multilevel models, e.g., hierarchical linear models*

No

Is a distinction made between dependent and independent variables?

Yes

No

go to page 21

Is there more than one dependent variable?

Yes

No

go to page 26

Is your dependent variable (a) intervally scaled, (b) not a dichotomy, and (c) noncontinuous or limited in range?

Yes

No

Limited dependent variable analysis**

go to page 28

*See multilevel models in the Glossary.

**See limited dependent variable in the Glossary.

● No distinction made between dependent and independent variables

Do you want to measure agreement?

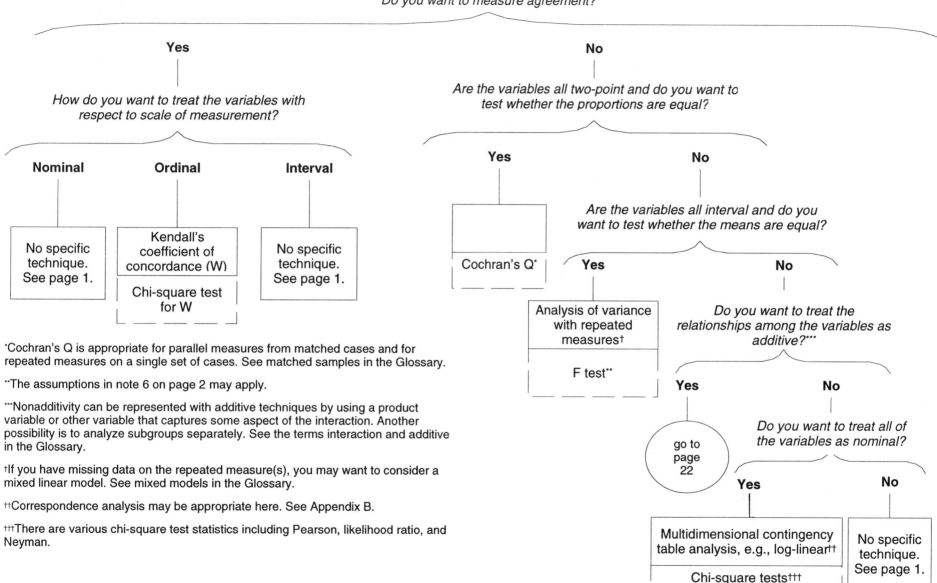

Yes

How do you want to treat the variables with respect to scale of measurement?

Nominal

No specific technique. See page 1.

Ordinal

Kendall's coefficient of concordance (W)

Chi-square test for W

Interval

No specific technique. See page 1.

No

Are the variables all two-point and do you want to test whether the proportions are equal?

Yes

Cochran's Q*

No

Are the variables all interval and do you want to test whether the means are equal?

Yes

Analysis of variance with repeated measures†

F test**

No

*Do you want to treat the relationships among the variables as additive?***

Yes

go to page 22

No

Do you want to treat all of the variables as nominal?

Yes

Multidimensional contingency table analysis, e.g., log-linear††

Chi-square tests†††

No

No specific technique. See page 1.

---

*Cochran's Q is appropriate for parallel measures from matched cases and for repeated measures on a single set of cases. See matched samples in the Glossary.

**The assumptions in note 6 on page 2 may apply.

***Nonadditivity can be represented with additive techniques by using a product variable or other variable that captures some aspect of the interaction. Another possibility is to analyze subgroups separately. See the terms interaction and additive in the Glossary.

†If you have missing data on the repeated measure(s), you may want to consider a mixed linear model. See mixed models in the Glossary.

††Correspondence analysis may be appropriate here. See Appendix B.

†††There are various chi-square test statistics including Pearson, likelihood ratio, and Neyman.

MORE THAN TWO VARIABLES (continued from page 21)

● No distinction made between dependent and independent variables ● Agreement is not to be measured ● The variables are not all two-point and a test of equal proportions is desired ● The variables are not all interval and a test of equal means is desired ● Relationships are to be treated as additive

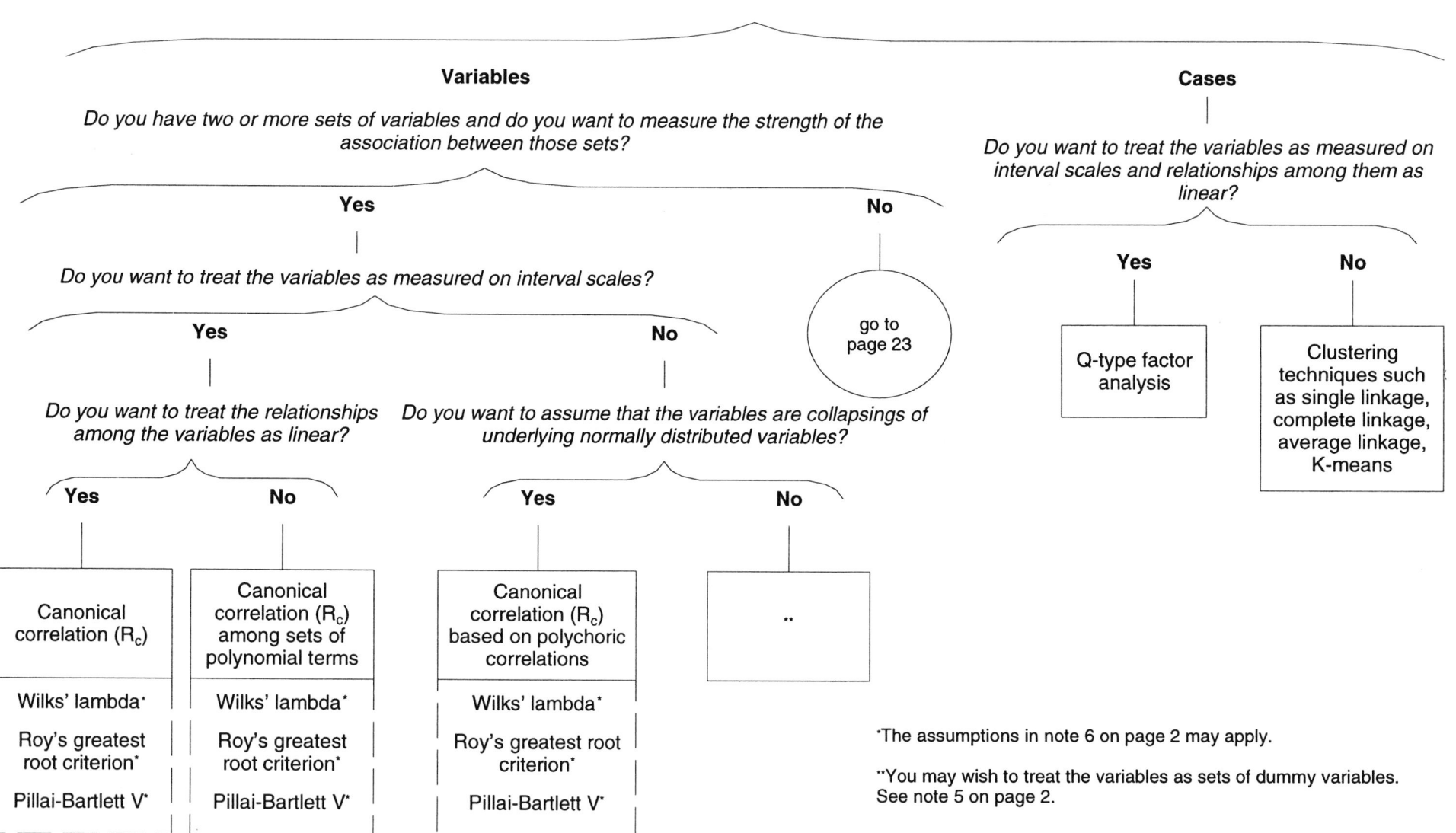

Do you want to analyze patterns existing among variables or among individual cases (e.g., persons)?

Variables

Do you have two or more sets of variables and do you want to measure the strength of the association between those sets?

Yes   **No**

Do you want to treat the variables as measured on interval scales?

Yes   **No**

Do you want to treat the relationships among the variables as linear?

Yes   **No**

Do you want to assume that the variables are collapsings of underlying normally distributed variables?

Yes   **No**

go to page 23

Cases

Do you want to treat the variables as measured on interval scales and relationships among them as linear?

Yes   **No**

| Q-type factor analysis | Clustering techniques such as single linkage, complete linkage, average linkage, K-means |

Canonical correlation (R_c)	Canonical correlation (R_c) among sets of polynomial terms	Canonical correlation (R_c) based on polychoric correlations	**
Wilks' lambda*	Wilks' lambda*	Wilks' lambda*	
Roy's greatest root criterion*	Roy's greatest root criterion*	Roy's greatest root criterion*	
Pillai-Bartlett V*	Pillai-Bartlett V*	Pillai-Bartlett V*	

*The assumptions in note 6 on page 2 may apply.

**You may wish to treat the variables as sets of dummy variables. See note 5 on page 2.

MORE THAN TWO VARIABLES (continued from page 22)

● No distinction is made between dependent and independent variables ● Agreement is not to be measured ● The variables are not all two-point and a test of proportions is desired   ● The variables are not all interval and a test of equal means is desired   ● Relationships are to be treated as additive ● Patterns among variables are to be analyzed ● Association between two or more sets of variables is not to be measured

Does the analysis involve two or more groups of individuals or cases?

Yes

No

go to page 24

Do you want to explore the relationships among a set of variables in two or more groups simultaneously or do you want to compare the similarity of the patterns of the relationships among a set of variables?

Explore Relationships

Compare Patterns

Do you want to treat all of the variables as interval and the relationships among them as linear?

Do you want to treat all of the variables as interval?

Yes

No

Yes

No

Do you want to preserve the metric units in which the variables were measured or to standardize them?

No specific technique. See page 1.

Three-mode factor analysis	Three-way non-metric multidimensional scaling techniques

Original Metric

Standardize

Multigroup confirmatory factor analysis of variance-covariance matrices

Maximum likelihood chi-square (χ^2)*

Multigroup confirmatory factor analysis of standardized variance-covariance matrices**

Maximum likelihood chi-square (χ^2)*

*The assumptions in note 6 on page 2 may apply.

**The variables should be standardized using the combined groups as a reference group. (This is not the same as using the correlation matrices for the separate groups.) See standardized variable in the Glossary.

MORE THAN TWO VARIABLES (continued from page 23)

● No distinction made between dependent and independent variables ● Relationships are to be treated as additive
● Patterns among variables are to be analyzed ● One group of individuals

Do you want to explore covariation among the variables (e.g., to examine their relationships to underlying dimensions) or do you want to find clusters of variables that are more strongly related to one another than to the remaining variables?

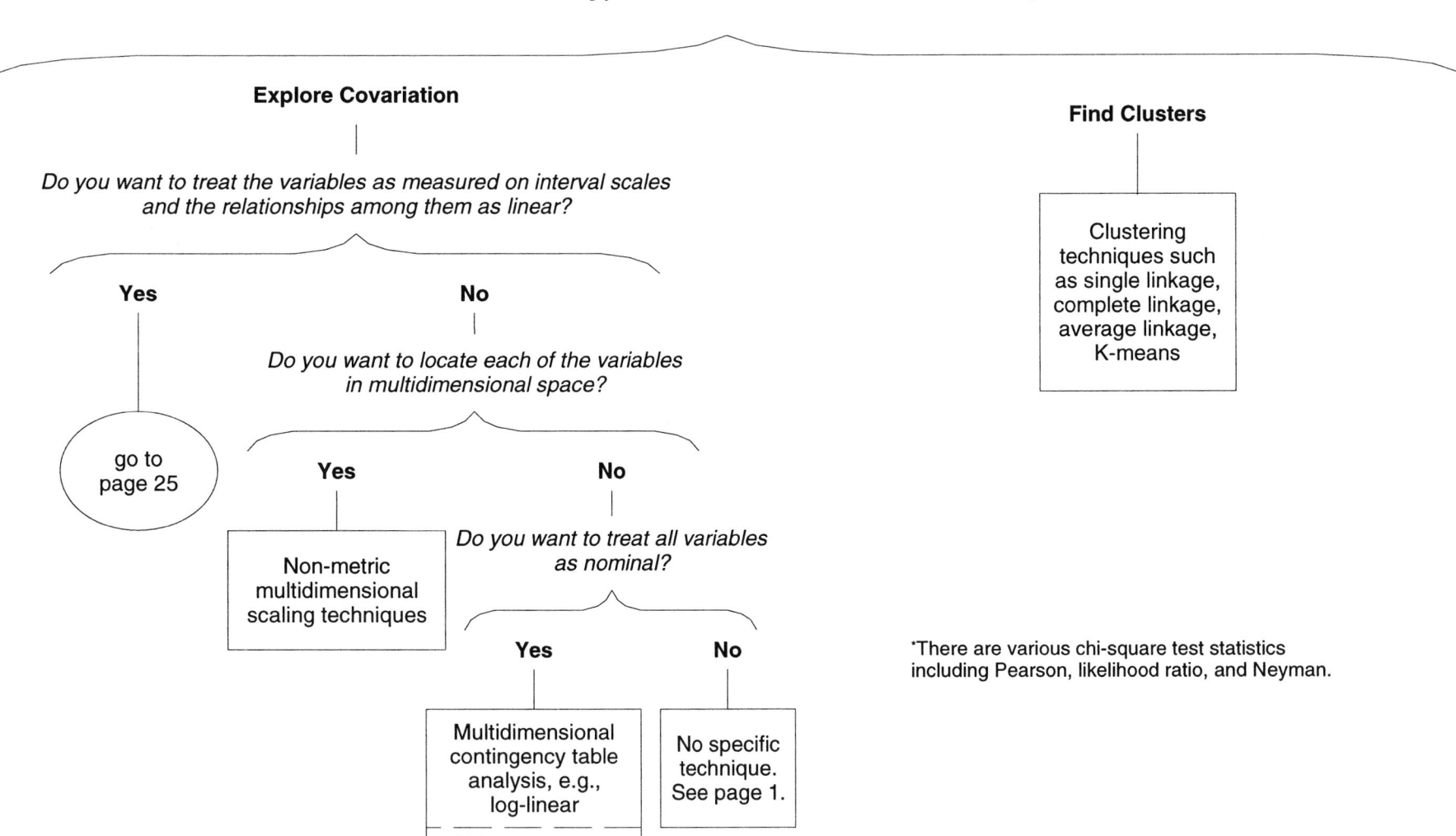

Explore Covariation

Do you want to treat the variables as measured on interval scales and the relationships among them as linear?

Yes

go to
page 25

No

Do you want to locate each of the variables in multidimensional space?

Yes

Non-metric
multidimensional
scaling techniques

No

Do you want to treat all variables as nominal?

Yes

Multidimensional
contingency table
analysis, e.g.,
log-linear

Chi-square tests*

No

No specific
technique.
See page 1.

Find Clusters

Clustering
techniques such
as single linkage,
complete linkage,
average linkage,
K-means

*There are various chi-square test statistics including Pearson, likelihood ratio, and Neyman.

● No distinction made between dependent and independent variables ● Relationships are to be treated as additive ● Patterns among variables are to be analyzed ● One group of individuals ● Covariation is to be explored ● The variables are to be treated as interval ● The relationships are to be treated as linear

Do you want to explore the relationships among the set of variables or do you want to compare the pattern of the relationships with a prespecified pattern?

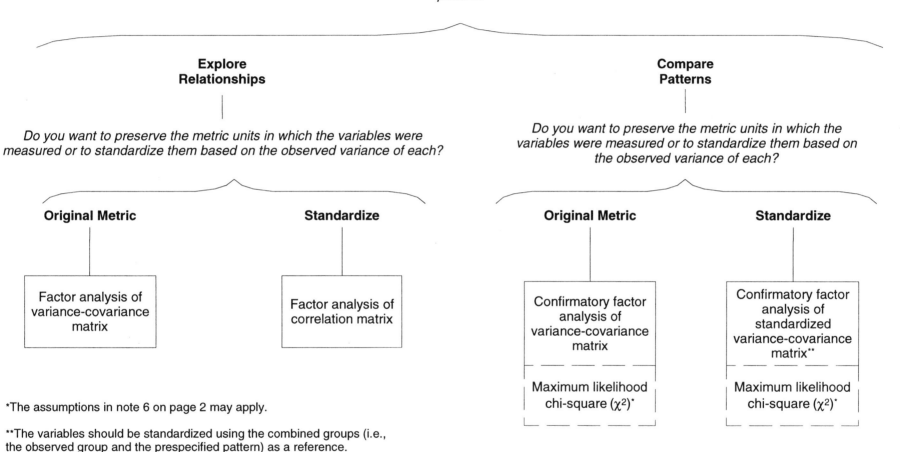

Explore Relationships

Do you want to preserve the metric units in which the variables were measured or to standardize them based on the observed variance of each?

Original Metric

Factor analysis of variance-covariance matrix

Standardize

Factor analysis of correlation matrix

Compare Patterns

Do you want to preserve the metric units in which the variables were measured or to standardize them based on the observed variance of each?

Original Metric

Confirmatory factor analysis of variance-covariance matrix

Maximum likelihood chi-square (χ^2)*

Standardize

Confirmatory factor analysis of standardized variance-covariance matrix**

Maximum likelihood chi-square (χ^2)*

*The assumptions in note 6 on page 2 may apply.

**The variables should be standardized using the combined groups (i.e., the observed group and the prespecified pattern) as a reference. (Depending on the pattern, this may or may not be equivalent to using the correlation matrix for the observed group.) See standardized variable in the Glossary.

MORE THAN TWO VARIABLES (continued from page 20)

● A distinction is made between dependent and independent variables ● There is more than one dependent variable

Do you want to treat all the dependent and independent variables as interval?

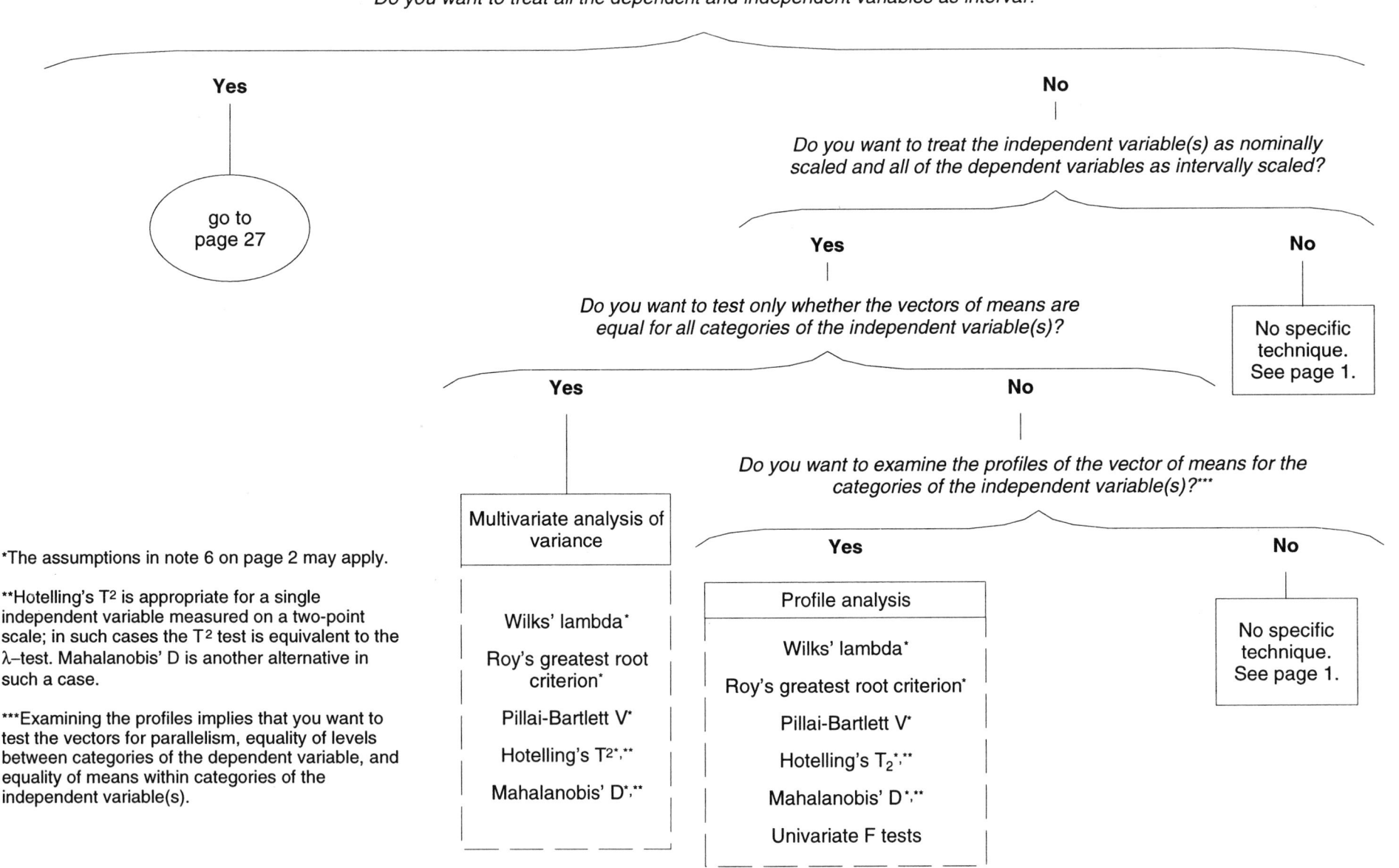

Yes

go to
page 27

No

*Do you want to treat the independent variable(s) as nominally
scaled and all of the dependent variables as intervally scaled?*

Yes

*Do you want to test only whether the vectors of means are
equal for all categories of the independent variable(s)?*

No

No specific
technique.
See page 1.

Yes

No

Multivariate analysis of
variance

Wilks' lambda*

Roy's greatest root
criterion*

Pillai-Bartlett V*

Hotelling's T²*,**

Mahalanobis' D*,**

*Do you want to examine the profiles of the vector of means for the
categories of the independent variable(s)?****

Yes

Profile analysis

Wilks' lambda*

Roy's greatest root criterion*

Pillai-Bartlett V*

Hotelling's T_2*,**

Mahalanobis' D*,**

Univariate F tests

No

No specific
technique.
See page 1.

*The assumptions in note 6 on page 2 may apply.

**Hotelling's T² is appropriate for a single
independent variable measured on a two-point
scale; in such cases the T² test is equivalent to the
λ–test. Mahalanobis' D is another alternative in
such a case.

***Examining the profiles implies that you want to
test the vectors for parallelism, equality of levels
between categories of the dependent variable, and
equality of means within categories of the
independent variable(s).

MORE THAN TWO VARIABLES (continued from page 26)

● A distinction is made between dependent and independent variables ● There is more than one dependent variable ● All variables are interval

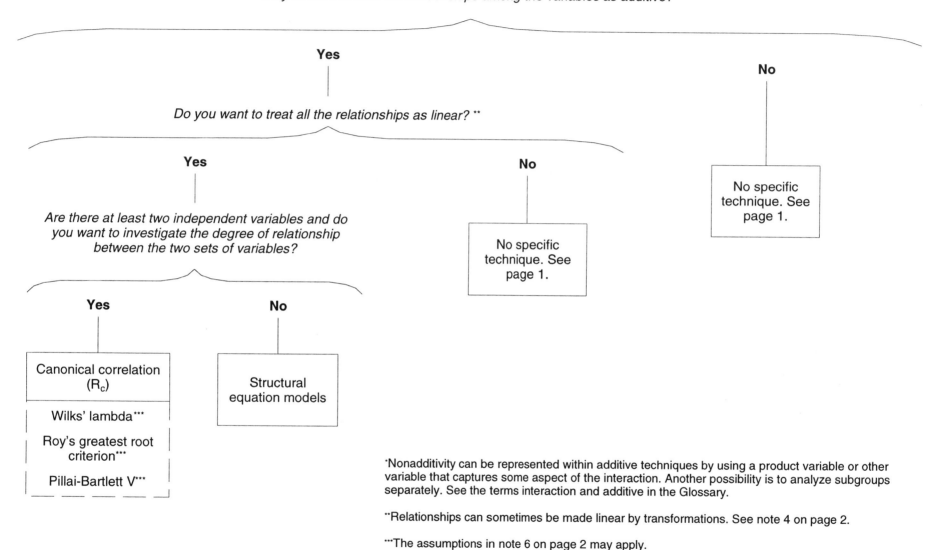

Do you want to treat the relationships among the variables as additive? ·

Yes

Do you want to treat all the relationships as linear? **

Yes

Are there at least two independent variables and do you want to investigate the degree of relationship between the two sets of variables?

Yes

Canonical correlation (R_c)

Wilks' lambda***

Roy's greatest root criterion***

Pillai-Bartlett V***

No

Structural equation models

No

No specific technique. See page 1.

No

No specific technique. See page 1.

·Nonadditivity can be represented within additive techniques by using a product variable or other variable that captures some aspect of the interaction. Another possibility is to analyze subgroups separately. See the terms interaction and additive in the Glossary.

**Relationships can sometimes be made linear by transformations. See note 4 on page 2.

***The assumptions in note 6 on page 2 may apply.

MORE THAN TWO VARIABLES (continued from page 20)

● A distinction is made between dependent and independent variables ● There is one dependent variable

Do you want to remove statistically the linear effects of one or more covariates from the dependent variable?

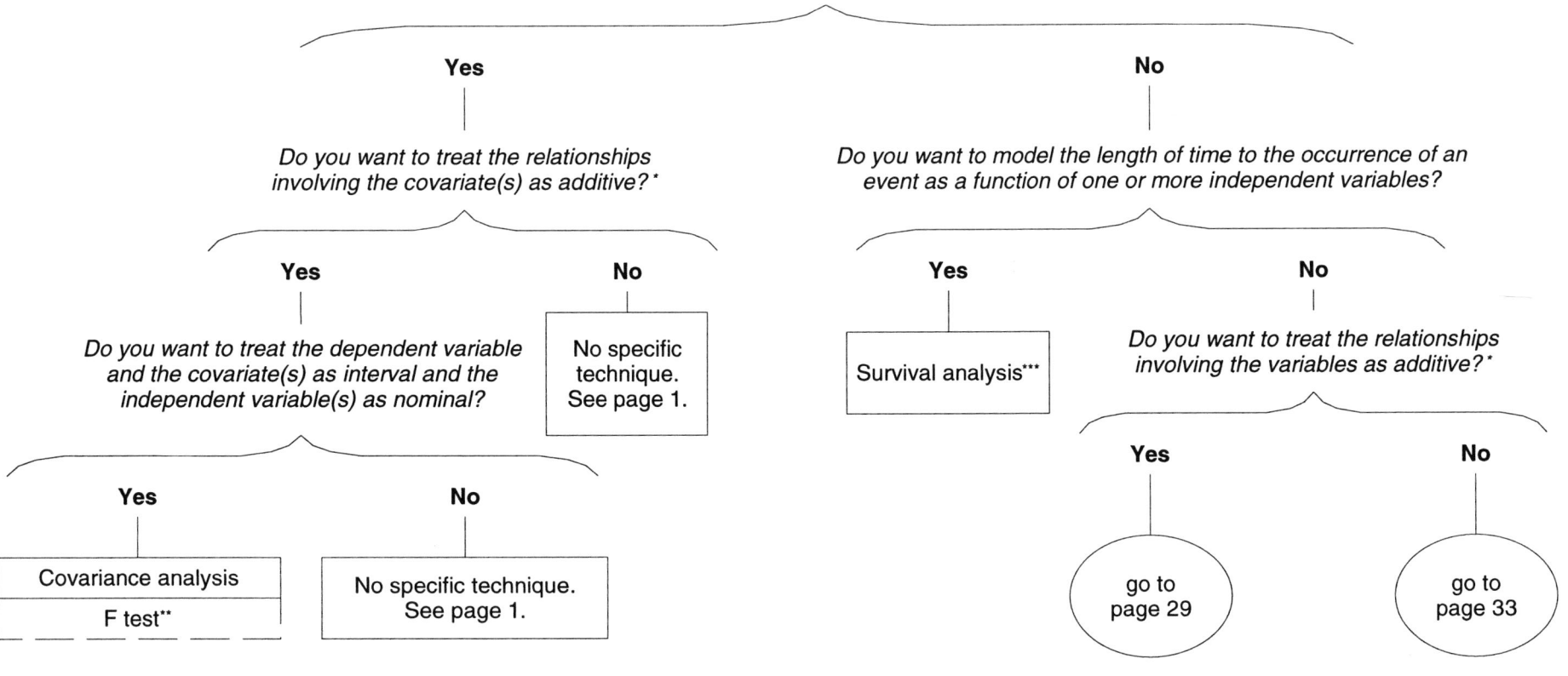

Yes

Do you want to treat the relationships involving the covariate(s) as additive? *

Yes

Do you want to treat the dependent variable and the covariate(s) as interval and the independent variable(s) as nominal?

Yes

Covariance analysis
F test**

No

No specific technique. See page 1.

No

No specific technique. See page 1.

No

Do you want to model the length of time to the occurrence of an event as a function of one or more independent variables?

Yes

Survival analysis***

No

Do you want to treat the relationships involving the variables as additive? *

Yes

go to page 29

No

go to page 33

*Nonadditivity can be represented with additive techniques by using a product variable or other variable that captures some aspect of the interaction. Another possibility is to analyze subgroups separately. See the terms interaction and additive in the Glossary.

**The assumptions in note 6 on page 2 may apply.

***Survival analysis is sometimes referred to as failure time analysis or event history analysis. It allows for censored data.

● A distinction is made between dependent and independent variables ● There is one dependent variable ● No covariate is used to remove linear effects ● Relationships among the variables are to be treated as additive

How do you want to treat the dependent variable with respect to measurement?

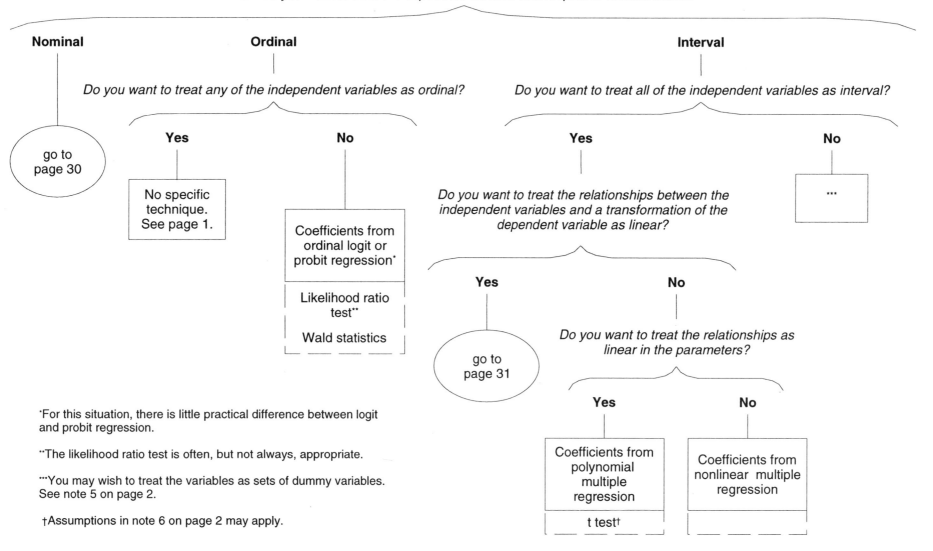

Nominal

go to page 30

Ordinal

Do you want to treat any of the independent variables as ordinal?

Yes

No specific technique. See page 1.

No

Coefficients from ordinal logit or probit regression*

Likelihood ratio test**

Wald statistics

Interval

Do you want to treat all of the independent variables as interval?

Yes

Do you want to treat the relationships between the independent variables and a transformation of the dependent variable as linear?

Yes

go to page 31

No

Do you want to treat the relationships as linear in the parameters?

Yes

Coefficients from polynomial multiple regression

t test†

No

Coefficients from nonlinear multiple regression

No

...

*For this situation, there is little practical difference between logit and probit regression.

**The likelihood ratio test is often, but not always, appropriate.

***You may wish to treat the variables as sets of dummy variables. See note 5 on page 2.

†Assumptions in note 6 on page 2 may apply.

MORE THAN TWO VARIABLES (continued from page 29)

● A distinction is made between dependent and independent variables ● There is one dependent variable ● No covariate is used to remove linear effects ● Relationships among the variables are to be treated as additive ● The dependent variable is nominal

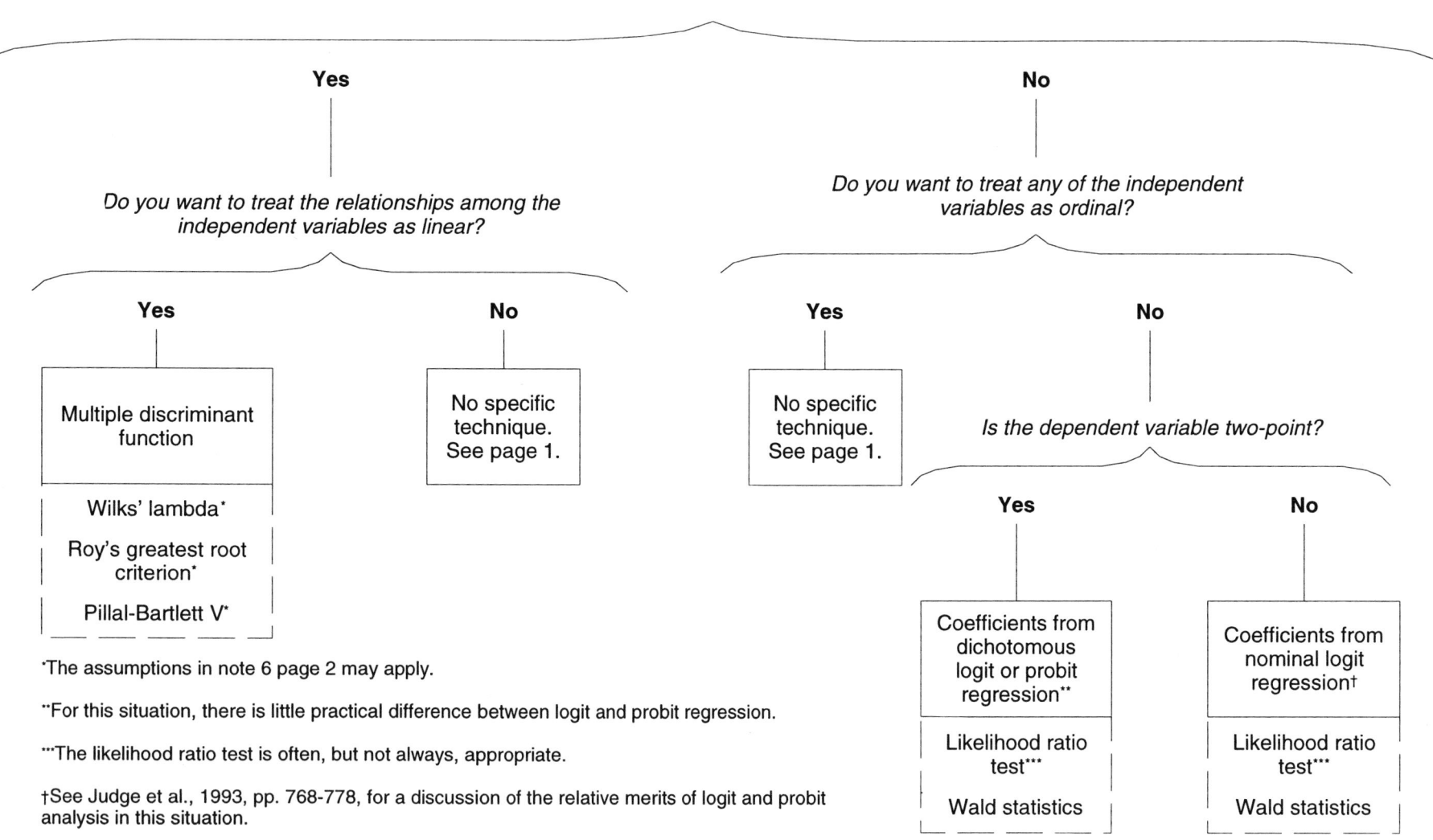

Do you want to treat all the independent variables as interval?

Yes

Do you want to treat the relationships among the independent variables as linear?

Yes

Multiple discriminant function

Wilks' lambda*

Roy's greatest root criterion*

Pillal-Bartlett V*

No

No specific technique. See page 1.

No

Do you want to treat any of the independent variables as ordinal?

Yes

No specific technique. See page 1.

No

Is the dependent variable two-point?

Yes

Coefficients from dichotomous logit or probit regression**

Likelihood ratio test***

Wald statistics

No

Coefficients from nominal logit regression†

Likelihood ratio test***

Wald statistics

*The assumptions in note 6 page 2 may apply.

**For this situation, there is little practical difference between logit and probit regression.

***The likelihood ratio test is often, but not always, appropriate.

†See Judge et al., 1993, pp. 768-778, for a discussion of the relative merits of logit and probit analysis in this situation.

MORE THAN TWO VARIABLES (continued from page 29)

● A distinction is made between dependent and independent variables ● There is one dependent variable ● No covariate is used to remove linear effects ● Relationships among the variables are to be treated as additive and linear ● All the variables are interval

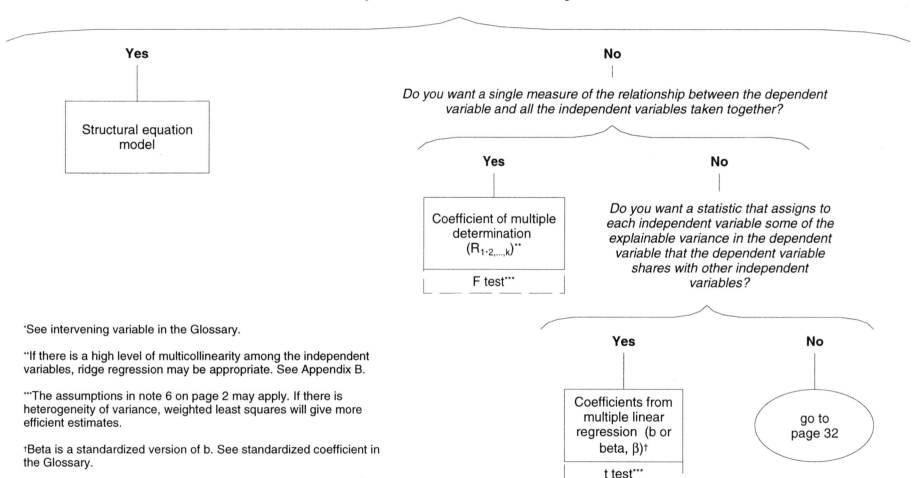

Does the analysis include at least one intervening variable? *

Yes

Structural equation model

No

Do you want a single measure of the relationship between the dependent variable and all the independent variables taken together?

Yes

Coefficient of multiple determination $(R_{1 \cdot 2, \ldots, k})$ **

F test ***

No

Do you want a statistic that assigns to each independent variable some of the explainable variance in the dependent variable that the dependent variable shares with other independent variables?

Yes

Coefficients from multiple linear regression (b or beta, β) †

t test ***

No

go to page 32

*See intervening variable in the Glossary.

**If there is a high level of multicollinearity among the independent variables, ridge regression may be appropriate. See Appendix B.

***The assumptions in note 6 on page 2 may apply. If there is heterogeneity of variance, weighted least squares will give more efficient estimates.

†Beta is a standardized version of b. See standardized coefficient in the Glossary.

MORE THAN TWO VARIABLES (continued from page 31)

● A distinction is made between dependent and independent variables ● There is one dependent variable ● No covariate is used to remove linear effects ● Relationships among the variables are to be treated as additive and linear ● All the variables are interval ● There is no intervening variable

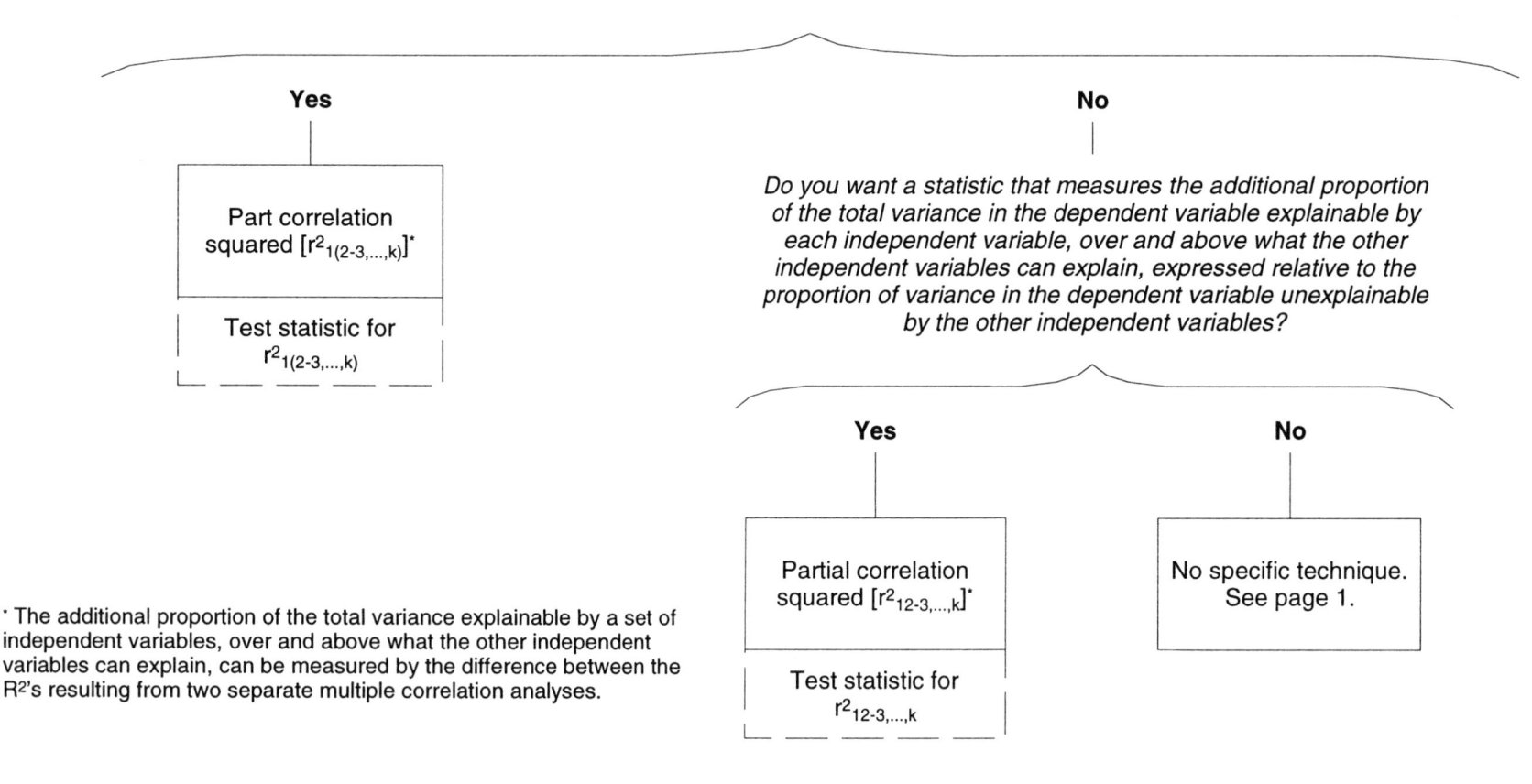

Do you want a statistic that measures the additional proportion of the total variance in the dependent variable explainable by each independent variable, over and above what the other independent variables can explain? ˙

Yes

Part correlation
squared [$r^2_{1(2\text{-}3,\ldots,k)}$]˙

Test statistic for
$r^2_{1(2\text{-}3,\ldots,k)}$

No

Do you want a statistic that measures the additional proportion of the total variance in the dependent variable explainable by each independent variable, over and above what the other independent variables can explain, expressed relative to the proportion of variance in the dependent variable unexplainable by the other independent variables?

Yes

Partial correlation
squared [$r^2_{12\text{-}3,\ldots,k}$]˙

Test statistic for
$r^2_{12\text{-}3,\ldots,k}$

No

No specific technique.
See page 1.

˙ The additional proportion of the total variance explainable by a set of independent variables, over and above what the other independent variables can explain, can be measured by the difference between the R^2's resulting from two separate multiple correlation analyses.

● A distinction is made between dependent and independent variables ● There is one dependent variable ● No covariate is used to remove linear effects ● Relationships among the variables are not to be treated as additive

Do you want to do an empirical search for strong relationships or to test a set of prespecified relationships?

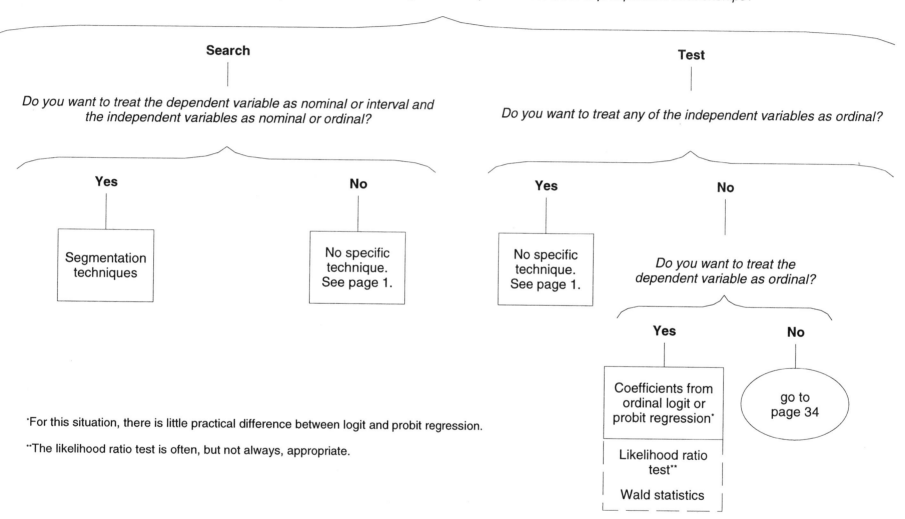

Search

Do you want to treat the dependent variable as nominal or interval and the independent variables as nominal or ordinal?

Yes

Segmentation techniques

No

No specific technique. See page 1.

Test

Do you want to treat any of the independent variables as ordinal?

Yes

No specific technique. See page 1.

No

Do you want to treat the dependent variable as ordinal?

Yes

Coefficients from ordinal logit or probit regression*

Likelihood ratio test**

Wald statistics

No

go to page 34

*For this situation, there is little practical difference between logit and probit regression.

**The likelihood ratio test is often, but not always, appropriate.

MORE THAN TWO VARIABLES (continued from page 33)

● A distinction is made between dependent and independent variables ● There is one dependent variable ● No covariate is used to remove linear effects ● Relationships among the variables are not to be treated as additive ● A set of prespecified relationships is to be tested ● No independent variable is to be treated as ordinal ●The dependent variable is not to be treated as ordinal

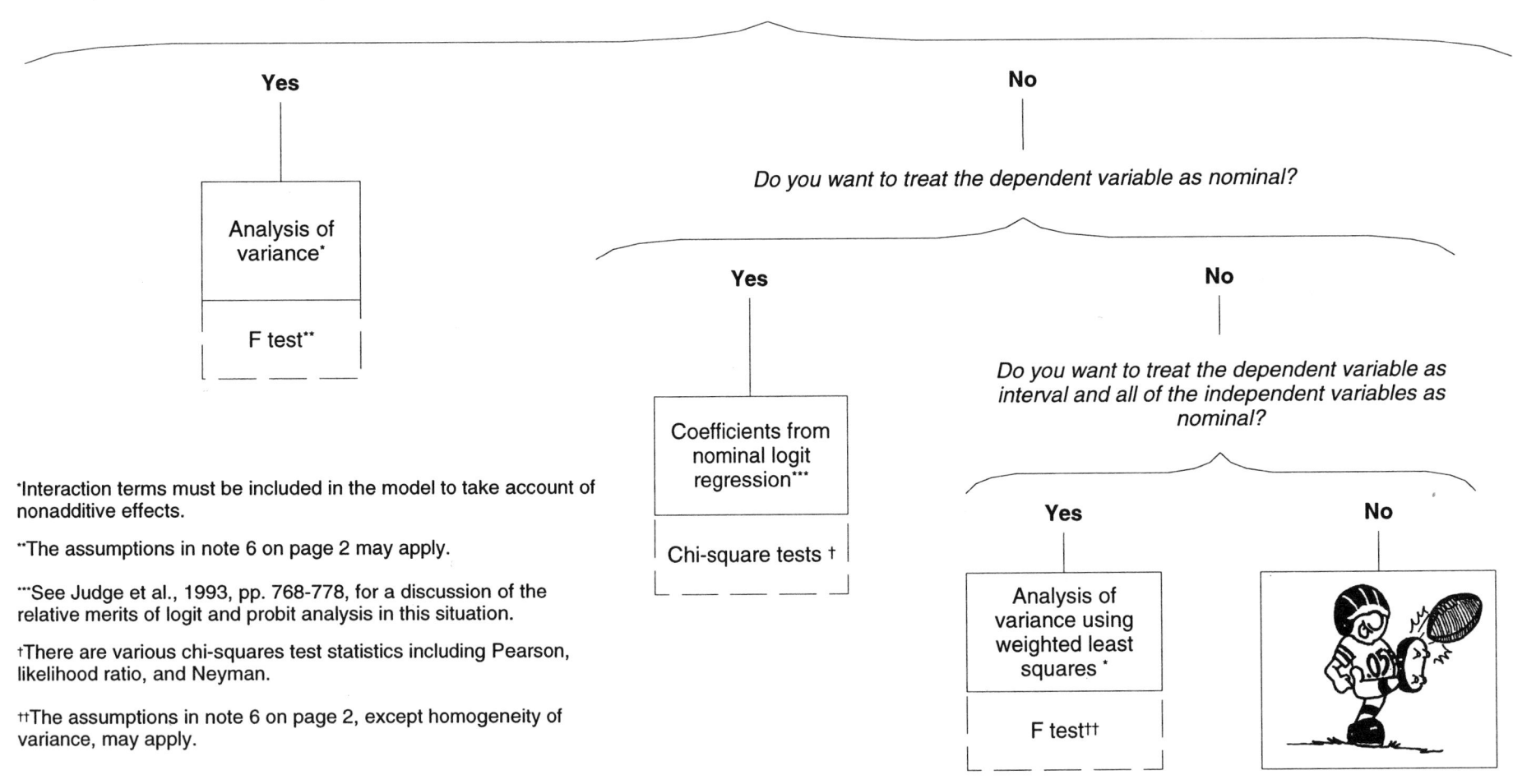

Do you want to treat the dependent variable as interval and all the independent variables as nominal, and do you want to assume homoscedasticity?

Yes

Analysis of variance*

F test**

No

Do you want to treat the dependent variable as nominal?

Yes

Coefficients from nominal logit regression***

Chi-square tests †

No

Do you want to treat the dependent variable as interval and all of the independent variables as nominal?

Yes

Analysis of variance using weighted least squares *

F test††

No

*Interaction terms must be included in the model to take account of nonadditive effects.

**The assumptions in note 6 on page 2 may apply.

***See Judge et al., 1993, pp. 768-778, for a discussion of the relative merits of logit and probit analysis in this situation.

†There are various chi-squares test statistics including Pearson, likelihood ratio, and Neyman.

††The assumptions in note 6 on page 2, except homogeneity of variance, may apply.

SAS IMPLEMENTATION

Where to Go in SAS to Find Statistics or Statistical Techniques Listed in the Decision Tree

For many of the statistics and statistical tests that appear in the Decision Tree, there exist one or more SAS procedures that calculate the statistic or test. The entries in this section are intended to guide you to an appropriate SAS procedure, macro, or technical support document to calculate the statistic or test. The procedures listed here are those that can be found in base SAS software, SAS/STAT software, or in SAS/INSIGHT software. If multiple procedures could be cited for a particular technique or test, the one(s) most readily providing the desired output is cited. No attempt was made to include all possible sources of information for each technique or test. SAS/INSIGHT is primarily listed for descriptive statistics and tests involving one variable, although there are many two-variable and multiple-variable techniques available through SAS/INSIGHT. The column labeled "Relevant Statements, Options, or Menu Choices" guides you in finding the desired information in the SAS documentation or in locating the appropriate menu choices in SAS/INSIGHT. Complete syntax is not included, nor is a detailed sequence of menu commands given. However, for SAS/INSIGHT, an attempt has been made to give sufficient menu options to enable you to find the statistic or test, based on the menu choices available in SAS software for Windows, Release 6.12. You will often find it helpful to read

the appropriate documentation or to explore the menu choices to find more detailed information. If SAS does not automatically calculate a certain statistic or test, limited information for the statistic or test is given in a footnote, where feasible. SAS is constantly being updated and augmented, so that more recent releases of SAS may contain different information on certain techniques or tests than that listed in the Implementation.

The releases of SAS that are included in the Implementation are 6.04, 6.08, 6.09, 6.10, 6.11, and 6.12. These releases (except 6.04 and 6.09) are available on the Windows platform. SAS/INSIGHT is available starting with Release 6.07 of SAS. To use SAS/INSIGHT, you must run SAS in interactive mode.

Release 6.04 documentation that has been used to prepare this guide includes: the *SAS Procedures Guide, Release 6.03 Edition*; the *SAS/STAT User's Guide, Release 6.03 Edition*; SAS Technical Report P-179, *Additional SAS/STAT Procedures, Release 6.03*; and SAS Technical Report P-20; *SAS/STAT Software: CALIS and LOGISTIC Procedures, Release 6.04*. For later releases of SAS: the *SAS Procedures Guide, Version 6, Third Edition* and *SAS/STAT User's Guide, Version 6, Fourth Edition,Volumes 1 and 2*, which includes SAS/STAT procedures through Release 6.06. For information on

SAS/STAT procedures that have been added or changed since Release 6.06, the excellent volume *SAS/STAT Software: Changes and Enhancements through Release 6.12* was used. Information on SAS/INSIGHT was based on the documentation in the *SAS/INSIGHT User's Guide, Version 6, Third Edition*.

You will also find especially helpful the following SAS publications in the Books by Users series: *Categorical Data Analysis Using the SAS System,* by Maura E. Stokes, Charles S. Davis, and Gary G. Koch; *Survival Analysis Using the SAS System: A Practical Guide*, by Paul D. Allison; and *SAS System for Mixed Models*, by Ramon C. Littell, George A. Milliken, Walter W. Stroup, and Russell D. Wolfinger.

Page	Technique or Test	SAS Procedure or Macro	Relevant Statements, Options, or Menu Choices	SAS Release					
				6.12	6.11	6.10	6.09	6.08	6.04
4	Mode	PROC FREQ*		●	●	●	●	●	●
	Relative frequency of classes	PROC FREQ		●	●	●	●	●	●
		PROC CHART	HBAR	●	●	●	●	●	●
	Relative frequencies, e.g., percentages	PROC FREQ		●	●	●	●	●	●
		PROC CHART	HBAR	●	●	●	●	●	●
		SAS/INSIGHT	Analyze: Distribution (Y): Output: Frequency table[†]	●	●	●	●	●	
	Absolute frequencies	PROC FREQ		●	●	●	●	●	●
		PROC CHART	HBAR	●	●	●	●	●	●
		SAS/INSIGHT	Analyze: Distribution (Y): Output: Frequency table[†]	●	●	●	●	●	
	Bar chart	PROC CHART	HBAR or VBAR	●	●	●	●	●	●
	Chi-square goodness-of-fit test	PROC FREQ[‡]	TABLES.../CHISQ	●					

*PROC FREQ will not specifically identify the mode, but will give the frequency and percent in each category of the nominal variable.

[†]SAS/INSIGHT will automatically generate a bar chart and a mosaic plot for nominal variables by using the Analyze: Distribution (Y) menu option. A frequency table will also be generated, if "frequency table" is selected from the output dialog box.

[‡]PROC FREQ gives a test for equal proportions in each category; to test for different proportions or frequencies, use the TESTF= or TESTP= options in the TABLES statement.

Page	Technique or Test	SAS Procedure or Macro	Relevant Statements, Options, or Menu Choices	SAS Release					
				6.12	6.11	6.10	6.09	6.08	6.04
4 (cont.)	Median	PROC UNIVARIATE		●	●	●	●	●	●
		SAS/INSIGHT	Analyze: Distribution(Y)	●	●	●	●	●	
	Inter-quartile range*	PROC UNIVARIATE		●	●	●	●	●	●
		SAS/INSIGHT	Analyze: Distribution(Y)	●	●	●	●	●	
	Quantiles	PROC UNIVARIATE	OUTPUT	●	●	●	●	●	●
5	Winsorized mean	SAS/INSIGHT	Analyze: Distribution(Y):Output	●	●	●	●	●	
	Trimmed mean	SAS/INSIGHT	Analyze: Distribution(Y):Output	●	●	●	●	●	
	Hampel estimate of location								
	Biweight mean								

*The inter-quartile range is labeled "Q3-Q1."

Page	Technique or Test	SAS Procedure or Macro	Relevant Statements, Options, or Menu Choices	SAS Release					
				6.12	6.11	6.10	6.09	6.08	6.04
5 (cont.)	Mean	PROC MEANS		●	●	●	●	●	●
		PROC UNIVARIATE		●	●	●	●	●	●
		SAS/INSIGHT	Analyze: Distribution(Y)	●	●	●	●	●	
	Median	PROC UNIVARIATE		●	●	●	●	●	●
		SAS/INSIGHT	Analyze: Distribution(Y)	●	●	●	●	●	
	Standard deviation	PROC MEANS		●	●	●	●	●	●
		PROC UNIVARIATE		●	●	●	●	●	●
		SAS/INSIGHT	Analyze: Distribution(Y)	●	●	●	●	●	
	Coefficient of variation	PROC MEANS	CV[*]	●	●	●	●	●	●
		PROC UNIVARIATE		●	●	●	●	●	●
		SAS/INSIGHT	Analyze: Distribution(Y)	●	●	●	●	●	

[*]The coefficient of variation is not generated by default in PROC MEANS. If statistics are requested in the PROC MEANS statement, all those desired must be listed.

Page	Technique or Test	SAS Procedure or Macro	Relevant Statements, Options, or Menu Choices	SAS Release					
				6.12	6.11	6.10	6.09	6.08	6.04
5 (cont.)	Range	PROC MEANS	RANGE*	●	●	●	●	●	●
		PROC UNIVARIATE		●	●	●	●	●	●
		SAS/INSIGHT	Analyze: Distribution(Y)	●	●	●	●	●	
	Inter-quartile Range[†]	PROC UNIVARIATE	PLOT	●	●	●	●	●	●
		SAS/INSIGHT	Analyze: Distribution(Y)	●	●	●	●	●	
	Box plot	PROC UNIVARIATE	PLOT	●	●	●	●	●	●
		SAS/INSIGHT	Analyze: BoxPlot/ MosaicPlot(Y)	●	●	●	●	●	
		SAS/INSIGHT	Analyze: Distribution(Y)	●	●	●	●	●	

*The range is not generated by default in PROC MEANS. If statistics are requested in the PROC MEANS statement, all those desired must be listed.

[†]The inter-quartile range is labeled "Q3-Q1."

Page	Technique or Test	SAS Procedure or Macro	Relevant Statements, Options, or Menu Choices	SAS Release					
				6.12	6.11	6.10	6.09	6.08	6.04
5 (cont.)	Skewness	PROC MEANS	SKEWNESS*	●	●	●	●	●	●
		PROC UNIVARIATE		●	●	●	●	●	●
		SAS/INSIGHT		●	●	●	●	●	
	Test statistic for skewness[†]								
	Kurtosis	PROC MEANS	KURTOSIS[‡]	●	●	●	●	●	●
		PROC UNIVARIATE		●	●	●	●	●	●
		SAS/INSIGHT	Analyze: Distribution(Y)	●	●	●	●	●	
	Test statistic for kurtosis[**]								

[*]Skewness is not generated by default in PROC MEANS. If statistics are requested in the PROC MEANS statement, all those desired must be listed.

[†]SAS does not calculate the standard error of skewness, but it may be calculated as square root of (6/n) for large samples sizes from a normal distribution.

[‡]Kurtosis is not generated by default in PROC MEANS. If statistics are requested in the PROC MEANS statement, all those desired must be listed.

[**]SAS does not calculate the standard error of kurtosis, but it may be calculated as square root of (24/n) for large samples sizes from a normal distribution.

Page	Technique or Test	SAS Procedure or Macro	Relevant Statements, Options, or Menu Choices	SAS Release					
				6.12	6.11	6.10	6.09	6.08	6.04
5 (cont.)	Relative frequencies, e.g., percentages	PROC FREQ		●	●	●	●	●	●
		PROC CHART	HBAR	●	●	●	●	●	●
		SAS/INSIGHT	Analyze: Distribution (Y): Output: Frequency table	●	●	●	●	●	
	Absolute frequencies	PROC FREQ		●	●	●	●	●	●
		PROC CHART	HBAR	●	●	●	●	●	●
		SAS/INSIGHT	Analyze: Distribution (Y): Output: Frequency table	●	●	●	●	●	
	Bar chart	PROC CHART	HBAR or VBAR	●	●	●	●	●	●
		SAS/INSIGHT	Analyze: Histogram/ Bar Chart (Y)	●	●	●	●	●	
	Histogram	PROC UNIVARIATE*	PLOT	●	●	●	●	●	●
		SAS/INSIGHT	Analyze: Histogram/ Bar Chart (Y)	●	●	●	●	●	
			Analyze: Distribution (Y)	●	●	●	●	●	

*PROC UNIVARIATE produces a stem and leaf plot for smaller sample sizes and a histogram for larger sample sizes.

Page	Technique or Test	SAS Procedure or Macro	Relevant Statements, Options, or Menu Choices	SAS Release					
				6.12	6.11	6.10	6.09	6.08	6.04
5 (cont.)	Stem and leaf plot	PROC UNIVARIATE*	PLOT	●	●	●	●	●	●
6	Kolmogorov-Smirnov one sample test	PROC UNIVARIATE†	NORMAL	●	●	●	●	●	●
		SAS/INSIGHT	Analyze: Distribution (Y): Output: Cumulative Distribution	●	●	●	●	●	
	Shapiro-Wilk test	PROC UNIVARIATE†	NORMAL	●	●	●	●	●	●
	Superimposition of normal density over histogram of your variable	SAS/INSIGHT	Analyze: Distribution (Y): Output: Density Estimation	●	●	●	●	●	
	Superimposition of cumulative normal distribution over cumulative distribution of your variable	SAS/INSIGHT	Analyze: Distribution (Y): Output: Cumulative Distribution	●	●	●	●	●	

*PROC UNIVARIATE produces a stem-and-leaf plot for smaller sample sizes and a histogram for larger sample sizes.

†PROC UNIVARIATE produces a Kolmogorov-Smirnov test for normality if the sample size is greater than 2000; a Shapiro-Wilk test is calculated for smaller sample sizes.

Page	Technique or Test	SAS Procedure or Macro	Relevant Statements, Options, or Menu Choices	SAS Release					
				6.12	6.11	6.10	6.09	6.08	6.04
6 (cont.)	Q-Q plot	SAS/INSIGHT	Analyze: Distribution (Y): Output	●	●	●	●	●	
		PROC UNIVARIATE*	PLOT	●	●	●	●	●	●
	Superimposition of particular density over histogram of your variable	SAS/INSIGHT	Analyze: Distribution (Y): Output: Density Estimation	●	●	●	●	●	
	Superimposition of cumulative particular distribution over cumulative distribution of your variable	SAS/INSIGHT	Analyze: Distribution (Y): Output: Cumulative Distribution	●	●	●	●	●	
	Chi-square goodness-of-fit test	PROC FREQ†	TABLES.../CHISQ	●					
7	Loglinear analysis	PROC CATMOD	LOGLIN	●	●	●	●	●	●

*PROC UNIVARIATE produces a normal probability plot, with asterisks for your data, and crosses for where the data would be if they were distributed normally.

†PROC FREQ gives a test for equal proportions in each category; to test for different proportions or frequencies, use the TESTF= or TESTP= option in the TABLES statement.

Page	Technique or Test	SAS Procedure or Macro	Relevant Statements, Options, or Menu Choices	SAS Release					
				6.12	6.11	6.10	6.09	6.08	6.04
7 (cont.)	Likelihood ratio test*	PROC CATMOD	ML	●	●	●	●	●	●
	Cohen's kappa	PROC FREQ	TABLES.../AGREE	●	●	●			
	Test statistic for kappa†	PROC FREQ	TABLES.../AGREE	●	●	●			
	McNemar test	PROC FREQ	TABLES.../AGREE	●	●	●			
	Goodman and Kruskal's gamma	PROC FREQ	TABLES.../MEASURES	●	●	●	●	●	●
	Phi	PROC FREQ	TABLES.../CHISQ	●	●	●	●	●	●
	Test statistic for gamma‡	PROC FREQ	TABLES.../MEASURES CL	●					
	Pearson chi-square	PROC FREQ	TABLES.../CHISQ	●	●	●	●	●	●
	Fisher's exact test	PROC FREQ	TABLES.../CHISQ**	●	●	●	●	●	●

*PROC CATMOD prints the likelihood ratio test, which is a goodness-of-fit test for the model. For a non-fully saturated model with two variables, this test is appropriate for the null hypothesis that the two variables are independent.

†SAS prints kappa and a 95% confidence interval; if the ALPHA= option is specified, a different confidence level can be specified.

‡No hypothesis test is printed, but SAS prints a 95% confidence interval for the statistic when the CL option is specified.

**For a 2x2 table, the CHISQ option on the TABLES statement will give Fisher's exact test. For tables that are larger than 2x2, the EXACT option must be used.

Page	Technique or Test	SAS Procedure or Macro	Relevant Statements, Options, or Menu Choices	SAS Release					
				6.12	6.11	6.10	6.09	6.08	6.04
7 (cont.)	Goodman and Kruskal's tau*	PROC FREQ	TABLES.../MEASURES	●	●	●	●	●	●
	Test statistic for tau[†]	PROC FREQ	TABLES.../MEASURES CL	●					
	Asymmetric lambda	PROC FREQ	TABLES.../MEASURES	●	●	●	●	●	●
	Test statistic for lambda[†]	PROC FREQ	TABLES.../MEASURES CL	●					
8	Contingency coefficient	PROC FREQ	TABLES.../CHISQ	●	●	●	●	●	●
	Pearson chi-square	PROC FREQ	TABLES.../CHISQ	●	●	●	●	●	●
	Cramer's V	PROC FREQ	TABLES.../CHISQ	●	●	●	●	●	●
	Symmetric lambda	PROC FREQ	TABLES.../MEASURES	●	●	●	●	●	●
	Test statistic for lambda[†]	PROC FREQ	TABLES.../MEASURES CL	●					
	Cohen's kappa	PROC FREQ	TABLES.../AGREE	●	●	●			

*PROC FREQ prints this as Kendall's tau b.

[†]No hypothesis test is printed, but SAS prints a 95% confidence interval for the statistic when the CL option is specified.

Page	Technique or Test	SAS Procedure or Macro	Relevant Statements, Options, or Menu Choices	SAS Release					
				6.12	6.11	6.10	6.09	6.08	6.04
8 (cont.)	Test statistic for kappa[*]	PROC FREQ	TABLES.../AGREE	●	●	●			
	Bowker's test[†]	PROC FREQ	TABLES.../AGREE	●	●	●			
9	Coefficient from monotone regression	PROC TRANSREG	MONOTONE	●	●	●	●	●	●
		PROC RANK, PROC REG[‡]		●	●	●	●	●	●
	Somers' d	PROC FREQ	TABLES.../MEASURES	●	●	●	●	●	●
	Test statistic for d[**]	PROC FREQ	TABLES.../MEASURES CL	●					
	Cohen's weighted kappa[††]	PROC FREQ	TABLES.../AGREE SCORES=	●	●	●			

[*]No test statistic is printed, but SAS prints a 95% confidence interval for kappa when the AGREE option is specified.

[†]Bowker's test (chi-square) is produced for square tables larger than 2x2; the p-value is automatically printed when the AGREE option is specified.

[‡]PROC RANK can be used to transform the observations for both variables into ranks, and then ordinary linear regression can be run on the ranked data, using PROC REG.

[**]No test statistic is printed, but SAS prints a 95% confidence interval for the statistic when the CL option is specified.

[††]Cohen's weighted kappa is automatically printed, along with simple kappa, when the AGREE option is used, and the table is at least a 3 x 3 table. To use weights other than the default weights, use the SCORES= option.

Page	Technique or Test	SAS Procedure or Macro	Relevant Statements, Options, or Menu Choices	SAS Release					
				6.12	6.11	6.10	6.09	6.08	6.04
9 (cont.)	Test statistic for weighted kappa[*]	PROC FREQ	TABLES.../AGREE SCORES=	●	●	●			
10	Spearman's rho	PROC FREQ	TABLES.../MEASURES	●	●	●	●	●	●
	Test statistic for rho[†]	PROC FREQ	TABLES.../MEASURES CL	●					
	Polychoric correlation[‡]	PROC FREQ	TABLES.../PLCORR	●	●	●			
	Likelihood ratio test								
	Pearson's product moment correlation (r)	PROC FREQ	TABLES.../MEASURES	●	●	●	●	●	●
	Test statistic for r	PROC FREQ	TABLES.../MEASURES EXACT	●					
	Mantel-Haenszel chi-square	PROC FREQ	TABLES.../CHISQ	●	●	●	●	●	●
	Kendall's tau a, tau b	PROC FREQ	TABLES.../MEASURES	●	●	●	●	●	●
	Goodman and Kruskal's gamma	PROC FREQ	TABLES.../MEASURES	●	●	●	●	●	●
	Stuart's tau c	PROC FREQ	TABLES.../MEASURES	●	●	●	●	●	●

[*]No test statistic for kappa or weighted kappa is printed, but a 95% confidence interval is printed.

[†]No hypothesis test is printed, but SAS prints a 95% confidence interval for the statistic when the CL option is specified.

[‡]For a 2x2 table, PROC FREQ prints the value as tetrachoric correlation.

Page	Technique or Test	SAS Procedure or Macro	Relevant Statements, Options, or Menu Choices	SAS Release 6.12	6.11	6.10	6.09	6.08	6.04
10 (cont.)	Test statistic for tau a, tau b, tau c or gamma[*]	PROC FREQ	TABLES.../MEASURES CL	●					
	Jonckheere-Terpstra test	PROC FREQ	TABLES.../JT EXACT	●					
11	Difference of means[†]	PROC MEANS		●	●	●	●	●	●
	t test for paired observations[†]	PROC MEANS	T PRT	●	●	●	●	●	●
	Intraclass correlation coefficient	%intracc macro		●	●	●	●	●	●
	F test[‡]								
	Krippendorff's coefficient of agreement								

[*] No hypothesis test is printed, but SAS prints a 95% confidence interval for the statistic when the CL option is specified.

[†] The difference of the two variables must first be calculated as a new variable in a DATA step. A test of whether the mean of this new variable = 0 is the same as a t test for paired observations done on the original two variables.

[‡] No F test or other test of significance is produced by the %intracc macro.

Page	Technique or Test	SAS Procedure or Macro	Relevant Statements, Options, or Menu Choices	SAS Release					
				6.12	6.11	6.10	6.09	6.08	6.04
12	Coefficient from dichotomous logit or probit regression	PROC LOGISTIC	LINK=LOGIT or LINK=PROBIT[*]	●	●	●	●	●	●
	Likelihood ratio test[†]	PROC LOGISTIC		●	●	●	●	●	●
	Wald statistic[‡]	PROC LOGISTIC		●	●	●	●	●	●
	Coefficients from polynomial logit or probit regression[**]	PROC LOGISTIC		●	●	●	●	●	●
	Coefficient(s) from nonlinear logit or probit regression	PROC NLIN		●	●	●	●	●	●
	Wald statistic[††]	PROC NLIN		●	●	●	●	●	●

[*]This option is LINK=NORMIT in Release 6.04 of the SAS software.

[†]The likelihood ratio test is printed as -2 log L in the Model Fitting and Global Null Hypothesis portion of the output. It is appropriate for testing the overall significance of the model.

[‡]The Wald chi-square is printed for the independent variable as part of the Analysis of Maximum Likelihood Estimates, and is appropriate for testing the null hypothesis that the individual parameter is zero.

[**]Polynomial terms for the independent variable must be created in a DATA step before being used in PROC LOGISTIC.

[††]Wald statistics are not produced by PROC NLIN, but it prints asymptotic standard errors and asymptotic 95% confidence intervals for the parameters.

Page	Technique or Test	SAS Procedure or Macro	Relevant Statements, Options, or Menu Choices	SAS Release					
				6.12	6.11	6.10	6.09	6.08	6.04
12 (cont.)	Coefficient from linear regression	PROC REG		●	●	●	●	●	●
	t test[*]	PROC REG		●	●	●	●	●	●
	Coefficients from polynomial regression[†]	PROC REG		●	●	●	●	●	●
	F test[‡]	PROC REG		●	●	●	●	●	●
	Coefficient(s) from nonlinear regression	PROC NLIN		●	●	●	●	●	●
13	Pearson's product moment correlation, r	PROC CORR		●	●	●	●	●	●
	Test statistic for r[**]	PROC CORR		●	●	●	●	●	●
	Biserial correlation, r_b								
	Test statistic for r_b								

[*]The t test is appropriate for testing the significance of each independent variable in the model.

[†]Polynomial terms for the independent variable must be created in a DATA step before being used in the regression.

[‡]The F test is appropriate for testing the overall significance of the model.

[**]PROC CORR does not print the test statistic for the correlation, but simply prints a p-value derived from the Fisher r to z transformation.

Page	Technique or Test	SAS Procedure or Macro	Relevant Statements, Options, or Menu Choices	SAS Release					
				6.12	6.11	6.10	6.09	6.08	6.04
13 (cont.)	Point biserial correlation (r_{pb})[*]	PROC CORR		●	●	●	●	●	●
	Test statistic for r_{pb}[*]	PROC CORR		●	●	●	●	●	●
	Tetrachoric correlation (r_t)[†]	PROC FREQ	TABLES.../ PLCORR	●	●	●			
	Test statistic for r_t[‡]	PROC FREQ	TABLES.../ PLCORR CL	●					
	Phi	PROC FREQ	TABLES.../ CHISQ	●	●	●	●	●	●
	Test statistic for phi[**]	PROC FREQ	TABLES.../CHISQ	●	●	●	●	●	●
14	Cochran-Armitage test	PROC FREQ	TABLES.../ TREND	●					
15	Sign Test	PROC UNIVARIATE[††]		●	●	●	●	●	●

[*]The point biserial correlation is equivalent to the Pearson product moment correlation.

[†]The PLCORR option produces the tetrachoric correlation when both variables are dichotomous.

[‡]No hypothesis test is printed, but SAS prints a 95% confidence interval for the statistic when the CL option is specified.

[**]The Pearson chi-square test is a test for phi = 0.

[††]The data must be arranged in SAS so that the values of the ordinal variable for matched cases are part of the same observations; then a new variable that is the difference between the matched values for the ordinal variable must be created. This new variable is the one that is analyzed in PROC UNIVARIATE.

Page	Technique or Test	SAS Procedure or Macro	Relevant Statements, Options, or Menu Choices	SAS Release					
				6.12	6.11	6.10	6.09	6.08	6.04
15 (cont.)	Wilcoxon signed ranks test	PROC UNIVARIATE[*]		●	●	●	●	●	●
	Friedman's chi-square test[†]	PROC FREQ	TABLES.../ CMH	●	●	●	●	●	●
	Coefficient from ordinal logit or probit regression	PROC LOGISTIC	LINK=LOGIT or LINK=PROBIT[‡]	●	●	●	●	●	●
	Somers' d	PROC FREQ	TABLES.../ MEASURES	●	●	●	●	●	●
	Likelihood ratio test[**]	PROC LOGISTIC		●	●	●	●	●	●
	Test statistic for Somers' d[††]	PROC FREQ	TABLES.../ MEASURES CL	●					

[*]The data must be arranged in SAS so that the values of the ordinal variable for matched cases are part of the same observations; then a new variable that is the difference between the matched values for the ordinal variable must be created. This new variable is the one that is analyzed in PROC UNIVARIATE.

[†]In order to obtain a Friedman's chi-square test in SAS, there must be three variables in the data set: one to identify the subject, another for the response, and another to identify the matched sample. The responses must first be ranked within each subject, and then analyzed in PROC FREQ; see pp. 887-888 of the *SAS/STAT User's Guide, Vol. 1* (1990).

[‡]This option is LINK=NORMIT in Release 6.04.

[**]The likelihood ratio test is printed as -2 log L in the Model Fitting and Global Null Hypothesis portion of the output.

[††]No hypothesis test is printed, but SAS prints a 95% confidence interval for the statistic when the CL option is specified.

Page	Technique or Test	SAS Procedure or Macro	Relevant Statements, Options, or Menu Choices	SAS Release					
				6.12	6.11	6.10	6.09	6.08	6.04
15 (cont.)	Median test	PROC NPAR1WAY	MEDIAN	●	●	●	●	●	●
	Mann-Whitney U test	PROC NPAR1WAY	WILCOXON	●	●	●	●	●	●
	Kolmogorov-Smirnov two sample test	PROC NPAR1WAY	EDF	●	●	●	●	●	●
	Runs test*								
	Freeman's coefficient of differentiation								
	Coefficients from ordinal logit or probit regression	PROC LOGISTIC†	LINK=LOGIT or LINK=PROBIT	●	●	●	●	●	●
	Kruskal-Wallis test	PROC NPAR1WAY	WILCOXON	●	●	●	●	●	●
	Median test (for more than 2 groups)	PROC NPAR1WAY	MEDIAN	●	●	●	●	●	●

*This test is available in PROC SHEWHART, which is part of SAS/QC software. It is not available in SAS/STAT.

†Check to be sure that the proportional odds assumption is met. (The chi-square test for the proportional odds assumption should be non-significant.) If the test is significant, you may need to use PROC CATMOD.

Page	Technique or Test	SAS Procedure or Macro	Relevant Statements, Options, or Menu Choices	SAS Release					
				6.12	6.11	6.10	6.09	6.08	6.04
15 (cont.)	Likelihood ratio test[*]	PROC LOGISTIC		●	●	●	●	●	●
	Wald statistics[†]	PROC LOGISTIC		●	●	●	●	●	●
16	Survival analysis[‡]	PROC LIFETEST		●	●	●	●	●	●
	Coefficients from nominal logit regression	PROC CATMOD		●	●	●	●	●	●
	Likelihood ratio test[**]	PROC CATMOD		●	●	●	●	●	●
	Wald statistics[††]	PROC CATMOD		●	●	●	●	●	●
	Eta^2								
	$Omega^2$								

[*]The likelihood ratio test is printed as -2 log L in the Model Fitting and Global Null Hypothesis portion of the output.

[†]The Wald chi-square is printed for the independent variable as part of the Analysis of Maximum Likelihood Estimates.

[‡]This assumes that you have two variables, one denoting time and the other status (i.e. censored or not). PROC LIFETEST will give estimates of median and mean survival time, plus product-limit estimates of survival, even when there are no explanatory variables.

[**]PROC CATMOD prints the likelihood ratio test, which is a goodness-of-fit test for the model.

[††]Wald statistics (chi-squares) are printed in the section titled Analysis of Weighted Least Squares Estimates, or Analysis of Maximum Likelihood Estimates.

Page	Technique or Test	SAS Procedure or Macro	Relevant Statements, Options, or Menu Choices	SAS Release					
				6.12	6.11	6.10	6.09	6.08	6.04
16 (cont.)	Intraclass correlation coefficient	%intracc macro		●	●	●	●	●	●
	Epsilon²								
	F test*								
17	Analysis of variance	PROC GLM		●	●	●	●	●	●
	F test	PROC GLM		●	●	●	●	●	●
	Difference of means	PROC TTEST		●	●	●	●	●	●
	t test†	PROC TTEST		●	●	●	●	●	●
	Welch statistic	PROC GLM	MEANS.../ WELCH‡	●					
	Bartlett's test**	PROC GLM	MEANS.../ HOVTEST=Bartlett	●					
	Levene's test**	PROC GLM	MEANS.../ HOVTEST=Levene	●					

*No F test or other test of significance is produced by the %intracc macro.

†PROC TTEST prints a test for homogeneity of variances in the two groups and two different t tests, one for equal and one for unequal variances.

‡PROC GLM will do Welch's variance-weighted, one-way anova when this option is specified. This test is robust to unequal within-group variances.

**PROC GLM will do additional tests for homogeneity of variance, including O'Brien's test and the Brown-Forsythe test.

Page	Technique or Test	SAS Procedure or Macro	Relevant Statements, Options, or Menu Choices	SAS Release					
				6.12	6.11	6.10	6.09	6.08	6.04
18	Analysis of variance	PROC GLM	MEANS.../ HOVTEST=Levene	●					
	Levene's test[*]	PROC GLM	MEANS.../ HOVTEST=Levene	●					
	Walsh test								
	Randomization test for matched pairs								
	Randomization test for matched samples								
	Randomization test for independent samples								
19	Coefficient from ordinal logit or probit regression	PROC LOGISTIC[†]	LINK=LOGIT or LINK=PROBIT[‡]	●	●	●	●	●	●

[*]PROC GLM will do additional tests for homogeneity of variance, including O'Brien's test and the Brown-Forsythe test.

[†]Check to be sure the proportional odds assumption is met; the chi-square test for the proportional odds assumption should be non-significant. If the test is significant, you may need to use PROC CATMOD.

[‡]This option is LINK=NORMIT in Release 6.04 of SAS software.

Page	Technique or Test	SAS Procedure or Macro	Relevant Statements, Options, or Menu Choices	SAS Release					
				6.12	6.11	6.10	6.09	6.08	6.04
19 (cont.)	Likelihood ratio test[*]	PROC LOGISTIC		●	●	●	●	●	●
	Wald statistic[†]	PROC LOGISTIC		●	●	●	●	●	●
	Polyserial correlation								
	Likelihood ratio test								
	Mayer and Robinson's M_{yu}								
	Test statistic for M_{yu}								
20	Multilevel models, e.g., hierarchical linear models	PROC MIXED		●	●	●	●	●	
	Limited dependent variable analysis[‡]	PROC GENMOD		●	●	●	●		
21	Kendall's coefficient of concordance (W)	PROC CORR	KENDALL	●	●	●	●	●	●

[*]The likelihood ratio test is printed as -2 log L in the Model Fitting and Global Null Hypothesis portion of the output.

[†]The Wald chi-square statistics are printed as part of the Analysis of Maximum Likelihood Estimates portion of the output.

[‡]PROC GENMOD can fit models for dependent variables that have a normal, binomial, or poisson distribution, among others. See the Glossary for a discussion of limited dependent variables.

Page	Technique or Test	SAS Procedure or Macro	Relevant Statements, Options, or Menu Choices	SAS Release					
				6.12	6.11	6.10	6.09	6.08	6.04
21 (cont.)	Chi-square test for W[*]	PROC CORR	KENDALL	●	●	●	●	●	●
	Cochran's Q	PROC FREQ	TABLES.../ AGREE	●	●	●			
	Analysis of variance with repeated measures	PROC GLM[†]	REPEATED	●	●	●	●	●	●
		PROC MIXED[‡]	REPEATED	●	●	●	●	●	
	F test	PROC GLM[**]	REPEATED	●	●	●	●	●	●
		PROC MIXED[††]	REPEATED	●	●	●	●	●	

[*]PROC CORR prints the p-value for the null hypothesis that $W=0$, but does not print the test statistic, which is based on a normal approximation.

[†] Data need to be structured so that repeated measures on the same subject are different variables within the same case. No missing data are allowed for any subject. If data are missing for any variable in the model, the entire case will be deleted from the analysis.

[‡]Data need to be structured so that all dependent variable values are in the same variable and another variable (e.g. time) indicates the level of the repeated variable. In this data structure, each subject or experimental unit would have more than one observation. Missing data can be handled in this procedure.

[**]PROC GLM assumes that the correlations between the observations on the same subject or experimental unit are all equal, and that all variances of the repeated measures are equal.

[††]PROC MIXED can estimate models with many different types of correlation structures between observations made on the same subject or experimental unit.

Page	Technique or Test	SAS Procedure or Macro	Relevant Statements, Options, or Menu Choices	SAS Release					
				6.12	6.11	6.10	6.09	6.08	6.04
21 (cont.)	Multidimensional contingency table analysis, e.g., log-linear*	PROC CATMOD	LOGLIN	●	●	●	●	●	●
	Chi-square tests	PROC CATMOD	LOGLIN	●	●	●	●	●	●
22	Canonical correlation	PROC CANCORR		●	●	●	●	●	●
	Wilks' lambda	PROC CANCORR		●	●	●	●	●	●
	Roy's greatest root criterion	PROC CANCORR		●	●	●	●	●	●
	Pillai-Bartlett V[†]	PROC CANCORR		●	●	●	●	●	●
	Canonical correlation among sets of polynomial terms[‡]	PROC CANCORR		●	●	●	●	●	●

*If correspondence analysis is used, the appropriate SAS procedure is PROC CORRESP.

[†]SAS prints this as Pillai's trace.

[‡]The polynomial terms must first be created in a DATA step, and then used in PROC CANCORR.

Page	Technique or Test	SAS Procedure or Macro	Relevant Statements, Options, or Menu Choices	SAS Release					
				6.12	6.11	6.10	6.09	6.08	6.04
22 (cont.)	Canonical correlation based on polychoric correlations[*]	%polychor macro, PROC CANCORR		●	●	●	●	●	●
	Q-type factor analysis	PROC TRANSPOSE, PROC FACTOR[†]		●	●	●	●	●	●
	Clustering techniques such as single linkage, complete linkage, average linkage, K-means	PROC CLUSTER[‡]		●	●	●	●	●	●
		PROC MODECLUS		●	●	●	●		
		PROC FASTCLUS		●	●	●	●	●	●
23	Three-mode factor analysis								
	Three-way non-metric multidimensional scaling techniques	PROC MDS		●	●	●	●	●	

[*]The %polychor macro may be used first to create a matrix of polychoric correlations, which are then analyzed using PROC CANCORR.

[†]Q-type factor analysis basically involves transposing the usual data matrix of cases (rows) by variables (columns) and doing a standard factor analysis on the cases. See Gorsuch (1983, p. 319) for details on how this should be implemented.

[‡]PROC CLUSTER has implemented the single linkage, average linkage, and centroid methods, among others; the K-means method is not implemented.

Page	Technique or Test	SAS Procedure or Macro	Relevant Statements, Options, or Menu Choices	SAS Release					
				6.12	6.11	6.10	6.09	6.08	6.04
23 (cont.)	Multigroup confirmatory factor analysis of variance-covariance matrices								
	Maximum likelihood chi-square								
	Multigroup confirmatory factor analysis of standardized variance-covariance matrices								
24	Non-metric multidimensional scaling techniques	PROC MDS		●	●	●	●	●	
	Multidimensional contingency table analysis, e.g., log-linear	PROC CATMOD	LOGLIN	●	●	●	●	●	●
	Chi-square tests	PROC CATMOD	LOGLIN	●	●	●	●	●	●

Page	Technique or Test	SAS Procedure or Macro	Relevant Statements, Options, or Menu Choices	SAS Release					
				6.12	6.11	6.10	6.09	6.08	6.04
24 (cont.)	Clustering techniques such as single linkage, complete linkage, average linkage, K-means	PROC CLUSTER*		●	●	●	●	●	●
		PROC MODECLUS†		●	●	●	●		
		PROC FASTCLUS		●	●	●	●	●	●
25	Factor analysis of variance-covariance matrix	PROC FACTOR	COVARIANCE	●	●	●	●	●	●
	Factor analysis of correlation matrix	PROC FACTOR		●	●	●	●	●	●
	Confirmatory factor analysis of variance-covariance matrix	PROC CALIS	COVARIANCE	●	●	●	●	●	●
	Maximum likelihood chi-square	PROC CALIS	COVARIANCE	●	●	●	●	●	●

*PROC CLUSTER has implemented the single linkage, average linkage, and centroid methods, among others; the K-means method is not implemented.

†PROC MODECLUS uses non-parametric clustering methods, which are capable of finding clusters of more generalized shapes than the roughly spherical ones found by PROC CLUSTER.

Page	Technique or Test	SAS Procedure or Macro	Relevant Statements, Options, or Menu Choices	SAS Release					
				6.12	6.11	6.10	6.09	6.08	6.04
25 (cont.)	Confirmatory factor analysis of standardized variance-covariance matrix	PROC CALIS		●	●	●	●	●	●
26	Multivariate analysis of variance	PROC GLM	MANOVA	●	●	●	●	●	●
	Wilks' lambda	PROC GLM	MANOVA	●	●	●	●	●	●
	Roy's greatest root criterion	PROC GLM	MANOVA	●	●	●	●	●	●
	Pillai-Bartlett V[*]	PROC GLM	MANOVA	●	●	●	●	●	●
	Hotelling's T^2								
	Mahalanobis' D								
	Profile analysis[†]	PROC GLM	REPEATED	●	●	●	●	●	●
	Wilks' lambda	PROC GLM	REPEATED	●	●	●	●	●	●
	Roy's greatest root criterion	PROC GLM	REPEATED	●	●	●	●	●	●

[*]PROC GLM prints this as Pillai's trace.

[†]The technique known as profile analysis can be analyzed as a repeated measures design in PROC GLM.

Page	Technique or Test	SAS Procedure or Macro	Relevant Statements, Options, or Menu Choices	SAS Release					
				6.12	6.11	6.10	6.09	6.08	6.04
26 (cont.)	Pillai-Bartlett V[*]	PROC GLM	REPEATED	●	●	●	●	●	●
	Hotelling's T^2								
	Mahalanobis' D								
	Univariate F tests[†]	PROC GLM	REPEATED	●	●	●	●	●	●
27	Canonical correlation	PROC CANCORR		●	●	●	●	●	●
	Wilks' lambda	PROC CANCORR		●	●	●	●	●	●
	Roy's greatest root criterion	PROC CANCORR		●	●	●	●	●	●
	Pillai-Bartlett V[*]	PROC CANCORR		●	●	●	●	●	●
	Structural equation models	PROC CALIS		●	●	●	●	●	●

[*]PROC GLM prints this as Pillai's trace.

[†]The univariate F tests in PROC GLM are based on the assumption of compound symmetry.

Page	Technique or Test	SAS Procedure or Macro	Relevant Statements, Options, or Menu Choices	SAS Release					
				6.12	6.11	6.10	6.09	6.08	6.04
28	Covariance analysis	PROC GLM*		●	●	●	●	●	●
	F test	PROC GLM		●	●	●	●	●	●
	Survival analysis	PROC LIFETEST†		●	●	●	●	●	
		PROC LIFEREG‡		●	●	●	●	●	●
		PROC PHREG**		●	●	●	●	●	●
		PROC LOGISTIC††		●	●	●	●	●	●

*The nominal independent variable(s) are given in a class statement in PROC GLM, and the covariate(s) are listed on the right hand side of the model statement. You may want to check for homogeneity of slopes by including interaction terms between the nominal variable(s) and the covariate(s). See *SAS System for Linear Models, Third Edition* for details.

†PROC LIFETEST produces an analysis of survival times, using the Product Limit, Kaplan-Meier, or Lifetable method, among others.

‡PROC LIFEREG produces an analysis of survival times, using parametric distributions, such as exponential, Weibull, logistic, and so on.

**PROC PHREG produces an analysis of survival times, using proportional hazards or Cox regression methods.

††PROC LOGISTIC can be used to analyze survival times measured in discrete intervals, rather than continuously. The data must be structured so that each interval in which a subject or experimental unit is observed is a separate case. See Allison (1995) for details.

Page	Technique or Test	SAS Procedure or Macro	Relevant Statements, Options, or Menu Choices	SAS Release					
				6.12	6.11	6.10	6.09	6.08	6.04
29	Coefficients from ordinal logit or probit regression	PROC LOGISTIC*	LINK=LOGIT or LINK=PROBIT	●	●	●	●	●	●
	Likelihood ratio test[†]	PROC LOGISTIC		●	●	●	●	●	●
	Wald statistic[‡]	PROC LOGISTIC		●	●	●	●	●	●
	Coefficients from polynomial multiple regression**	PROC REG		●	●	●	●	●	●
	t test	PROC REG		●	●	●	●	●	●
	Coefficients from nonlinear multiple regression	PROC NLIN		●	●	●	●	●	●

*Check to be sure the proportional odds assumption is met if the dependent variable has more than 2 levels. The chi-square test for the proportional odds assumption should be non-significant. If the test is significant, you may need to use PROC CATMOD, or check the model to see if additional terms (e.g. interaction) should be added.

[†]The likelihood ratio test is printed as -2 log L in the Model Fitting and Global Null Hypothesis portion of the PROC LOGISTIC output. It is appropriate for testing the significance of the overall model.

[‡]Wald statistics are used to test the significance of each coefficient in the model. They are printed as part of the Analysis of Maximum Likelihood Estimates in PROC LOGISTIC.

**Polynomial terms for the independent variable must be created in a DATA step before being used in PROC REG.

Page	Technique or Test	SAS Procedure or Macro	Relevant Statements, Options, or Menu Choices	SAS Release					
				6.12	6.11	6.10	6.09	6.08	6.04
30	Multiple discriminant function	PROC DISCRIM		●	●	●	●	●	●
	Wilks' lambda	PROC DISCRIM	MANOVA	●	●	●	●	●	●
	Roy's greatest root criterion	PROC DISCRIM	MANOVA	●	●	●	●	●	●
	Pillai-Bartlett V*	PROC DISCRIM	MANOVA	●	●	●	●	●	●
	Coefficients from dichotomous logit or probit regression	PROC LOGISTIC	LINK=LOGIT or LINK=PROBIT	●	●	●	●	●	●
	Likelihood ratio test[†]	PROC LOGISTIC		●	●	●	●	●	●
	Wald statistics[‡]	PROC LOGISTIC		●	●	●	●	●	●

[*]PROC DISCRIM prints this as Pillai's trace.

[†]The likelihood ratio test is printed as -2 log L in the Model Fitting and Global Null Hypothesis portion of the PROC LOGISTIC output. It is appropriate for testing the significance of the overall model.

[‡]Wald statistics are used to test the significance of each coefficient in the model. They are printed as part of the Analysis of Maximum Likelihood Estimates in PROC LOGISTIC.

Page	Technique or Test	SAS Procedure or Macro	Relevant Statements, Options, or Menu Choices	SAS Release					
				6.12	6.11	6.10	6.09	6.08	6.04
30 (cont.)	Coefficients from nominal logit regression	PROC CATMOD		●	●	●	●	●	●
	Likelihood ratio test*	PROC CATMOD		●	●	●	●	●	●
	Wald statistic†	PROC CATMOD		●	●	●	●	●	●
31	Structural equation model	PROC CALIS		●	●	●	●	●	●
	Coefficient of multiple determination, R‡	PROC REG		●	●	●	●	●	●
	F test	PROC REG		●	●	●	●	●	●
	Coefficients from multiple linear regression (b or beta)	PROC REG		●	●	●	●	●	●
	t test	PROC REG		●	●	●	●	●	●

*The likelihood ratio test in PROC CATMOD is a goodness-of-fit test for the model.

†Wald statistics are printed by PROC CATMOD as tests of the null hypothesis that the individual parameters = 0.

‡PROC REG prints R^2. You can calculate R by taking the square root of R^2.

Page	Technique or Test	SAS Procedure or Macro	Relevant Statements, Options, or Menu Choices	SAS Release					
				6.12	6.11	6.10	6.09	6.08	6.04
32	Part correlation squared[*]	PROC REG	SCORR2	●	●	●	●	●	●
	Test statistic for part correlation squared[†]								
	Partial correlation squared[‡]	PROC REG	PCORR2	●	●	●	●	●	●
	Test statistic for partial correlation squared[**]	PROC REG	PCORR2	●	●	●	●	●	●
33	Segmentation techniques	%treedisc macro		●	●	●	●	●	●
	Coefficients from ordinal logit or probit regression[††]	PROC LOGISTIC		●	●	●	●	●	●

[*]SAS calls this statistic the semi-partial correlation. There are two types of semi-partial correlations that are calculated (SCORR1 and SCORR2). Check the documentation for PROC REG for more information.

[†]SAS does not print a test for the part correlation squared (semi-partial correlation squared).

[‡]There are two types of squared partial correlations that are calculated (PCORR1 and PCORR2). Check the documentation for PROC REG for more information.

[**]The t test that is printed for testing the significance of each variable is appropriate for testing the significance of the partial correlation.

[††]Check to be sure the proportional odds assumption is met. The chi-square test for the proportional odds assumption should be non-significant. If the test is significant you may need to use PROC CATMOD, or check the model to see if additional terms (e.g., interaction) should be added.

Page	Technique or Test	SAS Procedure or Macro	Relevant Statements, Options, or Menu Choices	SAS Release					
				6.12	6.11	6.10	6.09	6.08	6.04
33 (cont.)	Likelihood ratio test*	PROC LOGISTIC		●	●	●	●	●	●
	Wald statistics†	PROC LOGISTIC		●	●	●	●	●	●
34	Analysis of variance	PROC GLM		●	●	●	●	●	●
	F test	PROC GLM		●	●	●	●	●	●
	Coefficients from nominal logit regression	PROC CATMOD		●	●	●	●	●	●
	Chi-square tests	PROC CATMOD		●	●	●	●	●	●
	Analysis of variance using weighted least squares	PROC GLM	WEIGHT	●	●	●	●	●	●
	F test	PROC GLM	WEIGHT	●	●	●	●	●	●

*The likelihood ratio test is printed as -2 log L in the Model Fitting and Global Null Hypothesis portion of the PROC LOGISTIC output. It is appropriate for testing the significance of the overall model.

†Wald chi-square statistics are printed as part of the Analysis of Maximum Likelihood Estimates in PROC LOGISTIC. They are used to test the significance of each coefficient in the model.

APPENDIX A

SOURCES OF FURTHER INFORMATION ABOUT
STATISTICS APPEARING IN THE GUIDE

Page 4

Mode	Hays, 1994, p. 165
Relative frequency of classes	Agresti and Finlay, 1986, p. 34, p. 47
Relative frequencies	Agresti and Finlay, 1986, p. 34
Absolute frequencies	Agresti and Finlay, 1986, p. 33
Bar chart	Hays, 1994, p. 90
Chi-square goodness-of-fit test	Siegel and Castellan, 1988, p. 45
Median	Hays, 1994, p. 166
Inter-quartile range	Agresti and Finlay, 1986, p. 46
Quantiles	Hays, 1994, p. 194

Page 5

Winsorized mean	Barnett and Lewis, 1994, p. 78
Trimmed mean	Barnett and Lewis, 1994, p. 78
Hampel estimate of location	Andrews et al., 1972, p. 2C3
Biweight mean	Mosteller and Tukey, 1977, p. 205
Mean	Hays, 1994, p. 168
Median	Hays, 1994, p. 166
Standard deviation	Hays, 1994, p. 183
Coefficient of variation	Snedecor and Cochran, 1989, p. 36
Range	Agresti and Finlay, 1986, p. 49
Inter-quartile range	Agresti and Finlay, 1986, p. 46
Box plot	Agresti and Finlay, 1986, p. 57
Skewness	Snedecor and Cochran, 1989, p. 79
Test statistic for skewness	Snedecor and Cochran, 1989, p. 80

Kurtosis	Snedecor and Cochran, 1989, p. 80
Test statistic for kurtosis	Snedecor and Cochran, 1989, p. 81
Relative frequencies	Agresti and Finlay, 1986, p. 34
Absolute frequencies	Agresti and Finlay, 1986, p. 33
Bar chart	Hays, 1994, p. 90
Histogram	Hays, 1994, p. 88
Stem and leaf plot	Agresti, 1986, p. 38

Page 6

Kolmogorov-Smirnov one-sample test	Siegel and Castellan, 1988, p. 51
Shapiro-Wilk test	Conover, 1980, p. 363
Superimposition of normal density over histogram of your variable	Hays, 1994, p. 109, p. 88
Superimposition of cumulative normal distribution over cumulative distribution of your variable	Hays, 1994, p. 111, p. 93
Q-Q plot	Snedecor and Cochran, 1989, p. 59
Superimposition of particular density over histogram of your variable	Hays, 1994, p. 109, p. 88
Superimposition of cumulative particular distribution over cumulative distribution of your variable	Hays, 1994, p. 111, p. 93
Chi-square goodness-of-fit test	Siegel and Castellan, 1988, p. 45

Page 7

Loglinear analysis	Agresti, 1990, p. 130
Likelihood ratio test	Agresti, 1990, p. 174
Cohen's kappa	Agresti, 1990, p. 365
Test statistic for kappa	Agresti, 1990, p. 366
McNemar's test	Agresti, 1990, p. 350

Goodman and Kruskal's gamma	Agresti, 1990, p. 22
Phi	Nunnally and Bernstein, 1994, p. 125
Test statistic for gamma	Agresti, 1990, p. 58
Pearson chi-square	Agresti, 1990, p. 47
Fisher's exact test	Agresti, 1990, p. 60
Goodman and Kruskal's tau	Agresti, 1990, p. 24
Test statistic for tau	Goodman and Kruskal, 1972, p. 417
Asymmetric lambda	Hays, 1994, p. 870
Test statistic for lambda	Hays, 1994, p. 872

Page 8

Contingency coefficient	Hays, 1994, p. 869
Pearson chi-square	Hays, 1994, p. 856
Cramer's V	Hays, 1994, p. 869
Symmetric lambda	Hays, 1994, p. 872
Test statistic for lambda	Hays, 1994, p. 872
Cohen's kappa	Agresti, 1990, p. 366
Test statistic for kappa	Agresti, 1990, p. 366
Bowker's test	Agresti, 1990, p. 354

Page 9

Coefficient from monotone regression	Conover, 1980, p. 272
Somers' d	Siegel and Castellan, 1988, p. 303
Test statistic for d	Siegel and Castellan, 1988, p. 307
Cohen's weighted kappa	Agresti, 1990, p. 367
Test statistic for weighted kappa	Fleiss, Cohen, and Everitt, 1969

Page 10

Spearman's rho	Siegel and Castellan, 1988, p. 235
Test statistic for r_s	Siegel and Castellan, 1988, p. 242

Polychoric correlation	Bollen, 1989, p. 441
Likelihood ratio test	Kleinbaum, Kupper, and Muller, 1988, p. 491
Pearson's product moment correlation	Hays, 1994, p. 609
Test statistic for r	Hays, 1994, p. 649
Mantel-Haenszel chi-square	Agresti, 1990, p. 283
Kendall's tau a	Agresti, 1984, p. 163
Kendall's tau b	Agresti, 1984, p. 161
Goodman and Kruskal's gamma	Agresti, 1984, p. 159
Stuart's tau c	Agresti, 1984, p. 177; Liebetrau, 1983, p. 72
Test statistic for tau a	Kendall, 1970, p. 51, p. 55
Test statistic for tau b	Liebetrau, 1983, p. 71
Test statistic for gamma	Liebetrau, 1983, p. 76
Test statistic for tau c	Liebetrau, 1983, p. 73
Jonckheere-Terpstra test	Siegel and Castellan, 1988, p. 216

Page 11

Difference of means	Hays, 1994, p. 338
t test for paired observations	Hays, 1994, p. 340
Intraclass correlation coefficient	Winer, Brown, and Michels, 1991, p. 93
F test	Winer, Brown, and Michels, 1991, p. 95
Krippendorff's coefficient of agreement	Krippendorff, 1970, p. 143

Page 12

Coefficient from dichotomous logit or probit regression	Hosmer and Lemeshow, 1989, p. 10; Agresti, 1996, p. 79 (brief discussion of probit models)
Likelihood ratio test	Hosmer and Lemeshow, 1989, p. 14; Agresti 1996, p. 79 (brief discussion of probit models)
Wald statistic	Hosmer and Lemeshow, 1989, p. 16; Agresti, 1996, p. 79 (brief discussion of probit models)

Coefficients from polynomial logit or probit regression	Neter, Wasserman, and Kutner, 1990, p. 578, p. 315
Coefficient(s) from nonlinear logit or probit regression	Neter, Wasserman, and Kutner, 1990, p. 578, p. 549
Coefficient from linear regression	Neter, Wasserman, and Kutner, 1990, p. 33
F test	Neter, Wasserman, and Kutner, 1990, p. 95
Coefficients from polynomial regression	Neter, Wasserman, and Kutner, 1990, p. 321
t test	Neter, Wasserman, and Kutner, 1990, p. 70, p. 326
Coefficient(s) from nonlinear regression	Neter, Wasserman, and Kutner, 1990, p. 549

Page 13

Pearson's product moment correlation	Hays, 1994, p. 609
Test statistic for r	Hays, 1994, p. 649
Biserial correlation	Nunnally and Bernstein, 1994, p. 126; McNemar, 1969, p. 215
Test statistic for r_b	McNemar, 1969, p. 217
Point biserial correlation	Nunnally and Bernstein, 1994, p. 125
Test statistic for r_{pb}	Hays, 1994, p. 649
Tetrachoric correlation	Nunnally and Bernstein, 1994, p. 126; McNemar, 1969, p. 221
Test statistic for r_t	McNemar, 1969, p. 223
Phi	Nunnally and Bernstein, 1994, p. 125
Test statistic for phi	Nunnally and Bernstein, 1994, p. 125; Hays, 1994, p. 649

Page 14

Cochran-Armitage test	Agresti, 1990, p. 100

Page 15

Sign test	Siegel and Castellan, 1988, p. 80
Wilcoxon signed-ranks test	Siegel and Castellan, 1988, p. 87
Friedman's chi-square test	Winer, Brown, and Michels, 1991, p. 1026
Coefficient from ordinal logit or probit regression	Agresti, 1984, p. 124; Agresti, 1996, p. 79 (brief discussion of probit models)
Somers' d	Agresti, 1984, p. 161; Liebetrau, 1983, p. 77
Likelihood ratio test	Agresti, 1984, p. 10
Test statistic for Somers' d	Liebetrau, 1983, p. 81
Median test	Siegel and Castellan, 1988, p. 124
Mann-Whitney U test	Conover, 1980, p. 215
Kolmogorov-Smirnov two-sample test	Siegel and Castellan, 1988, p. 144
Runs test	Siegel, 1956, p. 136
Freeman's coefficient of differentiation	Freeman, 1965, p. 112
Coefficients from ordinal logit or probit regression	Agresti, 1984, p. 124; Agresti, 1996, p. 79 (brief discussion of probit models)
Kruskal-Wallis test	Siegel and Castellan, 1988, p. 206
Median test (for more than two groups)	Siegel and Castellan, 1988, p. 200
Likelihood ratio test	Agresti, 1984, p. 10
Wald statistics	Agresti, 1990, p. 89

Page 16

Survival analysis	Yamaguchi, 1991
Coefficients from nominal logit regression	Agresti, 1990, p. 313
Likelihood ratio test	Agresti, 1990, p. 48, p. 313
Wald statistic	Agresti, 1990, p. 89

Eta^2	Winer, Brown, and Michels, 1991, p. 124
Omega^2	Winer, Brown, and Michels, 1991, p. 125
Intraclass correlation coefficient	Winer, Brown, and Michels, 1991, p. 126
Epsilon^2	Winer, Brown, and Michels, 1991, p. 124
F test	Winer, Brown, and Michels, 1991, p. 80

Page 17

Analysis of variance	Winer, Brown, and Michels, 1991, p. 74
F test	Winer, Brown, and Michels, 1991, p. 80
Difference of means	Winer, Brown, and Michels, 1991, p. 51
t test	Winer, Brown, and Michels, 1991, p. 66
Welch statistic	Brown and Forsythe, 1974
Bartlett's test	Winer, Brown, and Michels, 1991, p. 106
Levene's test	Snedecor and Cochran, 1989, p. 252

Page 18

Analysis of variance	Snedecor and Cochran, 1989, p. 217, p. 237
Levene's test	Snedecor and Cochran, 1989, p. 252
Walsh test	Siegel, 1956, p. 83
Randomization test for matched pairs	Snedecor and Cochran, 1989, p. 147
Randomization test for matched samples	Bradley, 1968, p. 80
Randomization test for independent samples	Snedecor and Cochran, 1989, p. 147 (for two independent samples); Bradley, 1968, p. 80

Page 19

Coefficient from ordinal logit or probit regression	Agresti, 1990, p. 318
Likelihood ratio test	Agresti, 1990, p. 48
Wald statistic	Agresti, 1990, p. 89

Q-type factor analysis   Gorsuch, 1983, p. 313
Clustering techniques   Sneath and Sokal, 1973; Aldenderfer and
                                                Blashfield, 1984

Page 23

Three-mode factor analysis   Gorsuch, 1983, p. 319
Three-way non-metric   Kruskal and Wish, 1978, p. 60
    multidimensional scaling techniques
Multigroup confirmatory factor   Bollen, 1989, p. 355; Jöreskog and Sörbom,
    analysis of variance-covariance   1989, p. 227
    matrices
Likelihood ratio test   Bollen, 1989, p. 361
Multigroup confirmatory factor   Bollen, 1989, p. 355; Jöreskog and Sörbom,
    analysis of standardized variance-   1989, p. 227 (see especially p. 238)
    covariance matrices

Page 24

Non-metric multidimensional scaling   Schiffman, Reynolds, and Young, 1981; Kruskal
    techniques   and Wish, 1978
Multidimensional contingency table   Agresti, 1990, p. 135
    analysis
Chi-square tests   Agresti, 1990, p. 47, p. 76
Clustering techniques   Sneath and Sokal, 1973; Aldenderfer and
                                                Blashfield, 1984

Page 25

Factor analysis of variance-covariance matrix	Gorsuch, 1983, p. 305
Factor analysis of correlation matrix	Gorsuch, 1983, p. 304
Confirmatory factor analysis of variance-covariance matrix	Bollen, 1989, p. 226
Likelihood ratio test	Bollen, 1989, p. 265
Confirmatory factor analysis of a standardized variance-covariance matrix	Bollen, 1989, p. 226

Page 26

Multivariate analysis of variance	Harris, 1985, p. 156; Bray and Maxwell, 1985
Wilks' lambda	Bray and Maxwell, 1985, p. 27
Roy's greatest root criterion	Bray and Maxwell, 1985, p. 27
Pillai-Bartlett V	Bray and Maxwell, 1985, p. 27
Hotelling's T^2	Harris, 1985, p. 99
Mahalanobis' D	Harris, 1985, p. 128
Profile analysis	Harris, 1985, p. 161
Univariate F tests	Winer, Brown, and Michels, 1991, p. 497, p. 526

Page 27

Canonical correlation	Harris, 1985, p. 200; Thompson, 1984
Wilks' lambda	Harris, 1985, p. 169, p. 212
Roy's greatest root criterion	Harris, 1985, p. 172, p. 212
Pillai-Bartlett V	Harris, 1985, p. 170, p. 212
Structural equation models	Bollen, 1989; Schumacker and Lomax, 1996

Page 28

Survival analysis	Yamaguchi, 1991
Covariance analysis	Neter, Wasserman, and Kutner, 1990, p. 861
F test	Neter, Wasserman, and Kutner, 1990, p. 99

Page 29

Coefficients from ordinal logit or probit regression	Agresti, 1984, p. 127; Agresti, 1996, p. 211, p. 216
Likelihood ratio test	Agresti, 1984, p. 10
Wald statistics	Agresti, 1990, p. 89
Coefficients from polynomial multiple regression	Neter, Wasserman, and Kutner, 1990, p. 329
t test	Neter, Wasserman, and Kutner, 1990, p. 326
Coefficients from nonlinear multiple regression	Neter, Wasserman, and Kutner, 1990, p. 549

Page 30

Multiple discriminant function	Harris, 1985, p. 167; Klecka, 1980
Wilks' lambda	Harris, 1985, p. 169
Roy's greatest root criterion	Harris, 1985, p. 172
Pillai-Bartlett V	Harris, 1985, p. 170
Coefficients from dichotomous logit or probit regression	Agresti, 1990, p. 85, p. 91
Likelihood ratio test	Agresti, 1990, p. 95
Wald statistics	Agresti, 1990, p. 89
Coefficients from nominal logit regression	Agresti, 1990, p. 307, p. 313

Page 31

Structural equation model	Bollen, 1989; Schumacker and Lomax, 1996
Coefficient of multiple determination	Neter, Wasserman, and Kutner, 1990, p. 241
F test	Neter, Wasserman, and Kutner, 1990, p. 240
Coefficients from multiple linear regression	Neter, Wasserman, and Kutner, 1990, p. 226 (b), p. 291 (β)
t test	Neter, Wasserman, and Kutner, 1990, p. 243

Page 32

Part correlation squared	Hays, 1994, p. 680
Test statistic for $r^2_{1(2\text{-}3,\ldots,k)}$	Hays, 1994, p. 684
Partial correlation squared	Hays, 1994, p. 674
Test statistic for $r^2_{1\cdot2\text{-}3,\ldots,k}$	Hays, 1994, p. 684

Page 33

Segmentation techniques	Fielding, 1977; Perreault and Barksdale, 1980
Coefficients from ordinal logit or probit regression	Agresti, 1984, p. 127 (see especially p. 130)
Likelihood ratio test	Agresti, 1984, p. 10
Wald statistics	Agresti, 1990, p. 89

Page 34

Analysis of variance	Neter, Wasserman, and Kutner, 1990, p. 673, p. 761, p. 818
F test	Neter, Wasserman, and Kutner, 1990, p. 707
Coefficients from nominal logit regression	Agresti, 1990, p. 307, p. 313
Chi-square tests	Agresti, 1990, p. 47, p. 76
Analysis of variance using weighted least squares	Neter, Wasserman, and Kutner, 1990, p. 363, p. 418
F test	Neter, Wasserman, and Kutner, 1990, p. 240

APPENDIX B

SOME STATISTICAL TECHNIQUES NOT INCLUDED IN THE GUIDE

There are many statistical techniques that are not included in this Guide, primarily because they do not fit well in the Guide structure. Some of these techniques are noted below.

1. Reduced variance regression techniques.

When you are predicting a dependent variable using two or more predictor variables, the appropriate weights to be applied to those predictor variables can be expected to show substantial variation from one random sample to another if the correlations among the predictor variables are high. Sometimes this is referred to as *instability of coefficients* that results from high multicollinearity among the predictor variables. In recent years there has been considerable discussion in the statistical literature about ways to achieve greater stability in regression coefficients by accepting certain biases. The underlying assumption is that it may be better to use coefficients that tend to be reasonably close to the ideal (population) value but, on average, tend to come out slightly different from this value, rather than a coefficient that averages to the correct value over many samples but that in any one sample may be very far off. A useful discussion of biased estimation techniques, including ridge regression, can be found in Judge et al. (1985, page 912ff).

2. Sampling errors of statistics from complex designs.

An assumption often required for the use of inferential statistics is that the observations are based on a simple random sample from some population. This assumption is required because the estimates of sampling error assume that each observation is independent of all others. Often, however, stratification or clustering is used instead of a simple random procedure, and this introduces nonindependence among the observations. Multilevel models can deal with these issues. In addition, there exist several special-purpose statistical software programs that can be used to estimate the sampling error of statistics from complex sampling designs. See Lee et al. (1989) for a discussion of analysis of complex survey data.

3. Time series analysis.

Generally, time series analysis uses regression techniques (often something other than ordinary least squares) to analyze or to predict change. Economists have been the leaders among social scientists in developing this area, but other social scientists increasingly are finding time series analysis to be relevant to their analytic problems. The Guide does not include time series analysis primarily because the decision-tree approach does not lend itself well to the analysis of data of a special type (which is the case with time series data). A discussion of time series analysis can be found in Judge et al. (1985, chapter 7) and Ostrom (1990).

4. Conjoint analysis.

Conjoint analysis refers to a class of techniques, particularly popular in market research, that are used to measure and analyze consumer preferences. A researched product or service is described by a *profile*, which is a combination of a particular level for each of several attributes. The technique is based on an assumption that subjects make decisions based on several factors simultaneously, or *jointly* -- hence the name conjoint. Carroll and Green (1995) provide an overview of recent developments in conjoint analysis.

5. Correspondence analysis.

Correspondence analysis is a "weighted principal component analysis of a contingency table" (*SAS/STAT User's Guide, Version 6, Fourth Edition*, p. 616). Usually, the analysis employs a table of frequencies of two (or more) categorical variables, and attempts to quantify columns (or rows) of the tables such that the between columns (or rows) sum of squares is maximized. Other terms for correspondence analysis include optimal scaling, reciprocal averaging, optimal scoring, appropriate scoring (United States); quantification method (Japan); homogeneity analysis (Netherlands); dual scaling (Canada); and scalogram analysis (Israel). Like conjoint analysis, correspondence analysis is particularly popular in market research (see Hoffman & Franke, 1986).

GLOSSARY OF SELECTED TERMS

additive A situation in which the best estimate of a dependent variable is obtained by simply adding together the appropriately computed effects of each of the independent variables. Additivity implies the absence of interactions. See also **interaction**.

agreement Agreement measures the extent to which two sets of scores (for example, scores obtained from two raters) are identical. Agreement involves a more stringent matching of two variables than does covariation, which implicitly allows one to change the mean (by adding a constant) and/or to change the variance (by multiplying by a constant) for either or both variables before checking the match.

bias The difference between the expected value of a statistic and the population value it is intended to estimate. See **expected value**.

bivariate normality A particular form of distribution of two variables that has the traditional "bell" shape (but not all bell-shaped distributions are normal). If plotted in three-dimensional space, with the vertical axis showing the number of cases, the shape would be that of a three-dimensional bell (if the variances on both variables were equal) or a "fireman's hat" (if the variances were unequal). When perfect bivariate normality obtains, the distribution of one variable is normal for each and every value of the other variable. See also **normal distribution**.

bracketing The operation of combining categories or ranges of values of a variable so as to produce a small number of categories. Sometimes referred to as *collapsing* or *grouping*.

capitalization on chance When one is searching for a maximally powerful prediction equation, chance fluctuations in a given sample increase the predictive power obtained; because data from another sample from the same population will show different chance fluctuations, the equation derived for one sample is likely to work less well in any other sample.

causal model An abstract quantitative representation of real-world dynamics (that is, of the causal dependencies and other interrelationships among observed or hypothetical variables).

censored data Data are said to be censored if certain values are not possible to observe. For example, an experiment on time to learning may end before all subjects have learned; or a study of length of unemployment may end before all participants have become employed.

complex sample design Any sample design that uses something other than simple random selection. Complex sample designs include multi-stage selection, and/or stratification, and/or clustering. For information on the calculation of sampling errors of statistics from complex designs, see note 2 in Appendix B.

compound symmetry Given multiple dependent variables, compound symmetry (or uniformity) requires that the population variances are equal and the population covariances are all equal (see Stevens, 1986, p. 412).

covariate A variable that is used in an analysis to correct, adjust, or modify the scores on a dependent variable before those scores are related to one or more independent variables. For example, in an analysis of how demographic factors (age, sex, education, etc.) relate to wage rates, monthly earnings might first be adjusted to take account of (that is, remove effects attributable to) number of hours worked, which in this example would be the covariate.

covariation Covariation is the extent to which two variables are associated, that is, the extent to which cases (for example, persons) have the same relative positions on two variables. See also **agreement**.

density function A function of a continuous random variable whose integral over an interval gives the probability that its value will fall within the interval. [Webster's Ninth New Collegiate Dictionary]. Synonym: probability density function.

dependent variable A variable that the analyst is trying to explain in terms of one or more independent variables. The distinction between dependent and independent variables is typically made on theoretical grounds, in terms of a particular causal model or to test a particular hypothesis. Synonym: criterion variable.

design matrix A specification, expressed in matrix format, of the particular effects and combinations of effects that are to be considered in an analysis.

dichotomous variable A variable that has only two categories. Gender (male/female) is an example. See also **two-point scale**.

dummy variable A variable with just two categories that reflects only part of the information actually available in a more comprehensive variable. For example, the four-category variable Region (Northeast, Southeast, Central, West) could be the basis for a two-category dummy variable that would distinguish Northeast from all other regions. Dummy variables often come in sets so as to reflect all of the original information. In our example, the four-category region variable defines four dummy variables: (1) Northeast vs. all other; (2) Southeast vs. all other; (3) Central vs. all other; and (4) West vs. all other. In an analysis of a variable with g categories, one would ordinarily use a set of $g-1$ dummy variables to capture all the information. Alternative coding procedures (which are equivalent in terms of explanatory power but which may produce more easily interpretable estimates) are effect coding and orthogonal polynomials.

expected value A theoretical average value of a statistic over an infinite number of samples from the same population.

heteroscedasticity The absence of homogeneity of variance. See **homogeneity of variance**.

homogeneity of variance A situation in which the variance on a dependent variable is the same (homogeneous) across all levels of the independent variables. In analysis of variance applications, several statistics are available for testing the homogeneity assumption (see Winer, Brown, and Michels, 1991, page 104); in regression applications, a lack of homogeneity can be detected by examination of residuals (see Neter, Wasserman, and Kutner, 1990, pages 120 and 423). In either case, a variance-stabilizing transformation may be helpful (see Snedecor and Cochran, 1989, page

286). Synonym: homoscedasticity. Antonym: heteroscedasticity.

homoscedasticity See **homogeneity of variance**.

independent variable A variable used to explain a dependent variable. Synonyms: predictor variable, explanatory variable. See also **dependent variable**.

interaction A situation in which the direction and/or magnitude of the relationship between two variables depends on (that is, differs according to) the value of one or more other variables. When interaction is present, simple additive techniques are inappropriate; hence, interaction is sometimes thought of as the absence of additivity. Synonyms: nonadditivity, conditioning effect, moderating effect, contingency effect. See also **product variable**.

interval scale A scale consisting of equal-sized units (dollars, years, etc.). On an interval scale, the distance between any two positions is of known size. Results from analytic techniques appropriate for interval scales will be affected by any non-linear transformation of the scale values. See also **scale of measurement**.

intervening variable A variable that is postulated to be a predictor of one or more dependent variables, and simultaneously predicted by one or more independent variables. Synonym: mediating variable.

kurtosis Kurtosis indicates the extent to which a distribution is more peaked or flat-topped than a normal distribution.

limited dependent variable A variable is said to be limited if certain values are not possible. Some of the causes may be censoring, truncating, or sample selection. See Breen (1996) for a discussion.

linear The form of a relationship among variables such that when any two variables are plotted, a straight line results. A relationship is linear if the effect on a dependent variable of a change of one unit in an independent variable is the same for all possible such changes.

matched samples Two (or more) samples selected in such a way that each case (for example, person) in one sample is matched -- that is, identical within specified limits -- on one or more preselected characteristics with a corresponding case in the other sample. One example of matched samples is having repeated measures on the same individuals. Another example is linking husbands and wives. Matched samples are different from independent samples, where such case-by-case matching on selected characteristics has not been assured.

measure of association A number (a statistic) whose magnitude indicates the degree of correspondence -- that is, strength of relationship -- between two variables. An example is the Pearson product-moment correlation coefficient. Measures of association are different from statistical tests of association (for example, Pearson chi-square, F test) whose primary purpose is to assess the probability that the strength of a relationship deviates from some predesigned value (often zero) by not more than would be expected due to the operation of chance if the cases studied were selected from a larger population. See also **statistical measure**, **statistical test**.

missing data Information that is not available for a particular case (for example, person) for which at least some other information is available. This can occur for a variety of reasons, including a person's refusal or inability to answer a question, nonapplicability of a question, etc. For a useful discussion of how to overcome problems caused by missing data in surveys, see Little and Rubin, 1989.

mixed models A mixed model is a generalization of the standard linear model in which both random and fixed effects are included. See also **multilevel models**.

multilevel models Social science data is often organized hierarchically; for example, students are nested within schools. Another common example is in a longitudinal panel design, with repeated observations nested within persons. Multilevel models allow one to model relationships within levels and across levels, and to deal with lack of independence among observations. Other terms sometimes used are *hierarchical linear models, mixed models, mixed-effect models, random-effects models, random-coefficient regression models,* and *variance components models.* See Bryk and Raudenbush (1992).

multivariate normality The form of a distribution involving more than two variables in which the distribution of one variable is normal for each and every combination of categories of all other variables. See Winer, Brown, and Michels (1991, pages 28 and 868) for a discussion of multivariate normality. See also **normal distribution**.

nominal scale A classification of cases that defines their equivalence and non-equivalence, but implies no quantitative relationships or ordering among them. Analytic techniques appropriate for nominally scaled variables are not affected by any one-to-one transformation of the numbers assigned to the classes. See also **scale of measurement**.

nonadditive Not additive. See **additive**, **interaction**.

normal distribution A particular form for the distribution of a variable that, when plotted, produces a bell-shaped symmetrical curve, rising smoothly from a small number of cases at both extremes to a large number of cases in the middle. Not all symmetrical bell-shaped distributions meet the definition of normality. See Hays (1994, page 237).

normality See **normal distribution**.

ordinal scale A classification of cases into a set of ordered classes such that each case is considered equal to, greater than, or less than every other case. Analytic techniques appropriate for ordinally scaled variables are not affected by any monotonic transformation of the numbers assigned to the classes. See also **scale of measurement**.

outlying case (outlier) A case (for example, person) whose score on a variable deviates substantially from the mean (or other measure of central tendency). Such cases can have disproportionately strong effects on statistics.

product variable An intervally scaled variable whose scores are equal to the product obtained when the values of two other variables are multiplied together. A product variable can be used to incorporate certain types of interaction in multivariate analysis.

quantile Any of several sets of possible values that divide the items of a frequency distribution into equally sized groups. Commonly used quantiles include: quartiles (4 groups); quintiles (5 groups); deciles (10 groups); and percentiles (100 groups).

ranks The position of a particular case (for example, person) relative to other cases on a defined scale-as in "1st place," "2nd place," etc. Note that when the actual values of the numbers designating the relative positions (the ranks) are used in analysis, they are being treated as an interval scale, not an ordinal scale. See also **interval scale, ordinal scale**.

scale of measurement As used in this Guide, scale of measurement refers to the nature of the assumptions one makes about the properties of a variable; in particular, whether that variable meets the definition of nominal, ordinal, or interval measurement. See also **nominal scale**, **ordinal scale**, **interval scale**.

segmentation techniques Segmentation techniques are model-free, exploratory procedures that algorithmically partition a set of observations into mutually exclusive and exhaustive subgroups. Typically, a data set is sequentially partitioned into subsets of observations, based on the categories of the independent variables. The decision about whether or how to partition is based on some criterion, for example, maximizing the between-groups sums of squares if the dependent variables are continuous. See Chaturvedi and Green (1995).

skewness Skewness is a measure of lack of symmetry of a distribution.

sphericity The sphericity condition is an assumption about the variances among the dependent variables in a situation with multiple dependent variables. Specifically, given k dependent variables and $(k-1)$ new orthogonal variables scaled such that sum of squares of the coefficients for each variable is 1.0, then those $(k-1)$ variables are *orthonormal* variables. The sphericity condition requires that the covariance matrix for the orthonormal variables be diagonal, with equal variances on the diagonal. See Stevens (1986, pages 412-413).

standardized coefficient When an analysis is performed on variables that have been standardized so that they have variances of 1.0, the estimates that result are known as standardized coefficients; for example, a regression run on original variables produces unstandardized regression coefficients known as b's, while a regression run on standardized variables produces standardized regression coefficients known as betas. In practice, both types of coefficients can be estimated from the original variables.

standardized variable A variable that has been transformed by multiplication of all scores by a constant and/or by the addition of a constant to all scores. Often these constants are selected so that the transformed scores have a mean of zero and a variance (and standard deviation) of 1.0.

statistical independence A complete lack of covariation between variables; a lack of association between variables. When used in analysis of variance or covariance, statistical independence between the independent variables is sometimes referred to as a balanced design.

statistical measure A number (a statistic) whose size indicates the magnitude of some quantity of interest, for example, the strength of a relationship, the amount of variation, the size of a difference, the level of income, etc. Examples include means, variances, correlation coefficients, and many others. Statistical measures are different from statistical tests. See also **statistical test**.

statistical test A number (a statistic) that can be used to assess the probability that a statistical measure deviates from some preselected value (often zero) by no more than would be expected due to the operation of chance if the cases (for example, persons) studied were randomly selected from a larger population. Examples include Pearson chi-square, F test, t test, and many others. Statistical tests are different from statistical measures. See also **statistical measure**.

test statistic A test statistic is used to test a finding for statistical significance. Examples are the t test, chi-square statistic, and F test. As used in this Guide, a test statistic often refers to the ratio of a particular statistic to the standard error of that statistic. This *critical ratio* can be referred to a z or t distribution to assess the probability that the statistic deviates from some preselected value (often zero) by no more than would be expected due to the operation of chance if the cases (for example, persons) studied were randomly selected from a larger population.

transformation A change made to the scores of all cases (for example, persons) on a variable by the application of the same mathematical operation(s) to each score. (Common operations include addition of a constant, multiplication by a constant, taking logarithms, ranking, bracketing, etc.)

two-point scale If each case is classified into one of two categories (for example, yes/no, male/female, dead/alive), the variable is a two-point scale. For analytic purposes, two-point scales can be treated as nominal scales, ordinal scales, or interval scales.

weighted data Weights are applied when one wants to adjust the impact of cases (for example, persons) in the analysis, for example, to take account of the number of population units that each case represents. In sample surveys, weights are most likely to be used with data derived from sample designs having different selection rates or with data having markedly different subgroup response rates.

REFERENCES

Agresti, A. (1984). *Analysis of Ordinal Categorical Data.* New York: Wiley.

Agresti, A. (1990). *Categorical Data Analysis.* New York: Wiley.

Agresti, A. (1996). *Introduction to Categorical Data Analysis.* New York: Wiley.

Agresti, A., & Finlay, B. (1986). *Statistical methods for the social sciences* (2nd ed.). San Francisco: Dellen.

Aldenderfer, M. S., and Blashfield, R. K. (1984). *Cluster Analysis.* Beverly Hills, CA: Sage.

Allison, P. D. (1995). *Survival Analysis Using the SAS System: A Practical Guide.* Cary, NC: SAS Institute Inc.

Andrews, D. F., Bickel, P. J., Hampel, F. R., Huber, P. J., Rogers, W. H., and Tukey, J. W. (1972). *Robust Estimates of Location: Survey and Advances.* Princeton: Princeton University Press.

Barnett, V.,and Lewis, T. (1994). *Outliers in Statistical Data* (3rd ed.). New York: Wiley.

Bollen, K. A. (1989). *Structural Equations with Latent Variables.* New York: Wiley.

Bradley, J. V. (1968). *Distribution-Free Statistical Tests.* Englewood Cliffs, NJ: Prentice-Hall.

Bray, J. H., and Maxwell, S. E. (1985). *Multivariate Analysis of Variance.* Beverly Hills, CA: Sage.

Breen, R. (1996). *Regression Models: Censored, Sample Selected, or Truncated Data.* Thousand Oaks, CA: Sage.

Brown, M. B., and Forsythe, A. B. (1974). The small sample behavior of some statistics which test the equality of several means. *Technometrics, 16,* 129-132.

Bryk, A. S. and Raudenbush, S. W. (1992). *Hierarchical Linear Models.* Thousand Oaks, CA: Sage.

Carroll, J. D., and Green, P. E. (1995). Psychometric methods in marketing research: Part I, conjoint analysis. *Journal of Marketing Research, 32,* 385-391.

Chaturvedi, A., and Green, P. E. (1995). Software review: SPSS for Windows, CHAID 6.0. *Journal of Marketing Research, 32,* 245-248.

Conover, W. J. (1980). *Practical Nonparametric Statistics* (2nd ed.). New York: Wiley.

Fielding, A. (1977). Binary segmentation: The Automatic Interaction Detector and related techniques for exploring data structures. In C. A. O'Muircheartaigh and C. Payne (Eds.), *The Analysis of Survey Data: Vol. 1, Exploring Data Structures* (pp. 221-257). New York: Wiley.

Fleiss, J. L., Cohen, J., and Everitt, B. S. (1969). Large sample standard errors of kappa and weighted kappa. *Psychological Bulletin, 72,* 323-327.

Freeman, L. C. (1965). *Elementary Applied Statistics for*

Students in Behavioral Science. New York: Wiley.

Goodman, L. A., and Kruskal, W. H. (1972). Measures of association for cross classification IV: Simplification of asymptotic variances. *Journal of the American Statistical Association, 67*, 415-421.

Gorsuch, R. L. (1983). *Factor Analysis* (2nd ed.). Philadelphia: W. B. Saunders.

Harris, R. J. (1985). *A Primer of Multivariate Statistics*. Orlando, FL: Academic Press.

Hays, W. L. (1994). *Statistics* (5th ed.). New York: Holt, Rinehart & Winston.

Hoffman, D. L., and Franke, G. R. (1986). Correspondence analysis: Graphical representation of categorical data in marketing research. *Journal of Marketing Research, 23*, 213-227.

Hosmer, D. W., Jr., and Lemeshow, S. (1989). *Applied Logistic Regression*. New York: Wiley.

Jöreskog, K. G., and Sörbom, D. (1989). *LISREL7: A Guide to the Program and Applications* (2nd ed.). Chicago IL: SPSS, Inc.

Judge, G. G., Griffiths, W. E., Hill, R. C., Lutkepohl, H., and Lee, T. (1985). *The Theory and Practice of Econometrics*. New York: Wiley.

Kendall, M. G. (1970). *Rank Correlation Methods* (4th ed.). London: Griffin.

Klecka, W. R. (1980). *Discriminant Analysis*. Beverly Hills, CA: Sage.

Kleinbaum, D. G., Kupper, L. L., and Muller, K. E. (1988). *Applied Regression Analysis and Other Multivariate Methods* (2nd ed.). Boston: PWS-Kent.

Krippendorf, K. (1970). Bivariate agreement coefficients for reliability of data. In E. F. Borgatta and G. W. Bohrnstedt (Eds.), *Sociological Methodology: 1970* (pp. 139-150). San Francisco: Jossey-Bass.

Kruskal, J. B., and Wish, M. (1978). *Multidimensional Scaling*. Beverly Hills, CA: Sage.

Lee, E. S., Forthofer, R. N., and Lorimor, R. J. (1989). *Analyzing Complex Survey Data*. Thousand Oaks, CA: Sage.

Liebetrau, A. M. (1983). *Measures of Association*. Beverly Hills, CA: Sage.

Littell, R. C., Milliken, G. A., Stroup, W., and Wolfinger, R. D. (1996). *SAS System for Mixed Models*. Cary, NC: SAS Institute Inc.

Little, R. J. A., and Rubin, D. B. (1989). The analysis of social science data with missing values. *Sociological Methods and Research, 18*, 292-326.

Maddala, G. S. (1983). *Limited-Dependent and Qualitative Variables in Econometrics*. Cambridge: Cambridge University Press.

Mayer, L. S., and Robinson, J. A. (1977). Measures of association for multiple regression models with ordinal predictor variables. In K. F. Schuessler (Ed.), *Sociological Methodology: 1978* (pp. 141-163). San Francisco: Jossey-Bass.

McNemar, Q. (1969). *Psychological Statistics* (4th ed.). New York: Wiley.

Mosteller, F., and Tukey, J. W. (1977). *Data Analysis and Regression*. Reading, MA: Addison-Wesley.

Neter, J., Wasserman, W., and Kutner, M. H. (1990).

Applied Linear Statistical Models (3rd ed.). Burr Ridge, IL: Irwin.

Nunnally, J. C., and Bernstein, I. H. (1994). *Psychometric Theory* (3rd ed.). New York: McGraw-Hill.

Olsson, U., Drasgow, F., and Dorans, N. J. (1982). The polyserial correlation coefficient. *Psychometrika, 47,* 337-347.

Ostrom, C. W. (1990). *Time Series Analysis: Regression Techniques* (2nd ed.). Thousand Oaks, CA: Sage.

Perreault, W. D., Jr., and Barksdale, H. C., Jr. (1980). A model-free approach for analysis of complex contingency data in survey research. *Journal of Marketing Research, 17,* 503-515.

SAS Institute Inc. (1988). *SAS Procedures Guide, Release 6.03 Edition.* Cary, NC: SAS Institute Inc.

SAS Institute Inc. (1988). SAS Technical Report P-179, *Additional SAS/STAT Procedures, Release 6.03.* Cary, NC: SAS Institute Inc.

SAS Institute Inc. (1988). *SAS/STAT User's Guide, Release 6.03 Edition.* Cary, NC: SAS Institute Inc.

SAS Institute Inc. (1990). SAS Technical Report P-200, *SAS/STAT Software: CALIS and LOGISTIC Procedures, Release 6.04.* Cary, NC: SAS Institute Inc.

SAS Institute Inc. (1990). *SAS/STAT User's Guide, Version 6, Fourth Edition, Volume 1.* Cary NC: SAS Institute Inc.

SAS Institute Inc. (1990). *SAS/STAT User's Guide, Version 6, Fourth Edition, Volume 2.* Cary NC: SAS Institute Inc.

SAS Institute Inc. (1995). *SAS/INSIGHT User's Guide, Version 6, Third Edition.* Cary NC: SAS Institute Inc.

SAS Institute Inc. (1997). *SAS/STAT Software: Changes and Enhancements through Release 6.12.* Cary, NC: SAS Institute Inc.

Schiffman, S. S., Reynolds, M. L., and Young, F. W. (1981). *Introduction to Multidimensional Scaling: Theory, Methods, and Applications.* New York: Academic Press.

Schumacker, R. E., and Lomax, R. G. (1996). *A Beginner's Guide to Structural Equation Modeling.* Mahwah, NJ: Erlbaum.

Siegel, S., and Castellan, N. J., Jr. (1988). *Nonparametric Statistics.* New York: McGraw-Hill.

Siegel, S. (1956). *Nonparametric Methods for the Behavioral Sciences.* New York: McGraw-Hill.

Sneath, P. H. A., and Sokal, R. R. (1973). *Numerical Taxonomy.* San Francisco: W. H. Freeman.

Snedecor, G. W., and Cochran, W. G. (1989). *Statistical Methods* (8th ed.). Ames, IA: Iowa State University Press.

Stevens, J. (1986). *Applied Multivariate Statistics for the Social Sciences.* Hillsdale, NJ: Erlbaum.

Stokes, M. E., Davis, C.S., and Koch, G. G. (1995). *Categorical Data Analysis Using the SAS System.* Cary, NC: SAS Institute Inc.

Thompson, B. (1984). *Canonical Correlation Analysis.* Beverly Hills, CA: Sage.

Winer, B. J., Brown, D. R., and Michels, K. M. (1991).

Statistical Principles in Experimental Design
(3rd ed.). New York: McGraw-Hill.

Yamaguchi, K. (1991). *Event History Analysis*. Newbury
Park, CA: Sage.

INDEX OF STATISTICS OR STATISTICAL TECHNIQUES
IN THE DECISION TREE OR IN APPENDIX B

BOOKS by USERS

SAS Institute's
Author Service

Call your local SAS® office to order these other books and tapes available through the Books by Users℠ program:

An Array of Challenges — Test Your SAS® Skills
by **Robert Virgile** .... Order No. A55625

Applied Multivariate Statistics with SAS® Software
by **Ravindra Khattree**
and **Dayanand N. Naik** .... Order No. A55234

Applied Statistics and the SAS® Programming Language, Fourth Edition
by **Ronald P. Cody**
and **Jeffrey K. Smith** .... Order No. A55984

Beyond the Obvious with SAS® Screen Control Language
by **Don Stanley** .... Order No. A55073

The Cartoon Guide to Statistics
by **Larry Gonick**
and **Woollcott Smith** .... Order No. A55153

Categorical Data Analysis Using the SAS® System
by **Maura E. Stokes, Charles E. Davis,**
and **Gary G. Koch** .... Order No. A55320

Common Statistical Methods for Clinical Research with SAS® Examples
by **Glenn A. Walker** .... Order No. A55991

Concepts and Case Studies in Data Management
by **William S. Calvert**
and **J. Meimei Ma** .... Order No. A55220

Essential Client/Server Survival Guide, Second Edition
by **Robert Orfali, Dan Harkey,**
and **Jeri Edwards** .... Order No. A56285

Extending SAS® Survival Analysis Techniques for Medical Research
by **Alan Cantor** .... Order No. A55504

A Handbook of Statistical Analysis using SAS
by **B.S. Everitt**
and **G. Der** .... Order No. A56378

The How-To Book for SAS/GRAPH® Software
by **Thomas Miron** .... Order No. A55203

In the Know ... SAS® Tips and Techniques From Around the Globe
by **Phil Mason** .... Order No. A55513

Learning SAS® in the Computer Lab
by **Rebecca J. Elliott** .... Order No. A55273

The Little SAS® Book: A Primer
by **Lora D. Delwiche**
and **Susan J. Slaughter** .... Order No. A55200

Mastering the SAS® System, Second Edition
by **Jay A. Jaffe** .... Order No. A55123

The Next Step: Integrating the Software Life Cycle with SAS® Programming
by **Paul Gill** .... Order No. A55697

Painless Windows 3.1: A Beginner's Handbook for SAS® Users
by **Jodie Gilmore** .... Order No. A55505

Painless Windows: A Handbook for SAS® Users
by **Jodie Gilmore** .... Order No. A55769

Professional SAS® Programming Secrets, Second Edition
by **Rick Aster**
and **Rhena Seidman** .... Order No. A56279

Professional SAS® User Interfaces
by **Rick Aster** .... Order No. A56197

Quick Results with SAS/GRAPH® Software
by **Arthur L. Carpenter**
and **Charles E. Shipp** .... Order No. A55127

Quick Start to Data Analysis with SAS®
by **Frank C. Dilorio**
and **Kenneth A. Hardy** .... Order No. A55550

Reporting from the Field: SAS® Software Experts Present Real-World Report-Writing Applications .... Order No. A55135

SAS® Applications Programming: A Gentle Introduction
by **Frank C. Dilorio** .... Order No. A55193

SAS® Foundations: From Installation to Operation
by **Rick Aster** .... Order No. A55093

SAS® Programming by Example
by **Ron Cody**
and **Ray Pass** .... Order No. A55126

SAS® Programming for Researchers and Social Scientists
by **Paul E. Spector** .... Order No. A56199

SAS® Software Roadmaps: Your Guide to
Discovering the SAS® System
by Laurie Burch
and SherriJoyce King ....Order No. A56195

SAS® Software Solutions
by Thomas Miron.................Order No. A56196

SAS® System for Elementary Statistical Analysis, Second Edition
by Sandra D. Schlotzhauer
and Dr. Ramon C. Littell ....Order No. A55172

SAS® System for Forecasting Time Series,
1986 Edition
by John C. Brocklebank
and David A. Dickey ....Order No. A5612

SAS® System for Linear Models, Third Edition
by Ramon C. Littell, Rudolf J. Freund,
and Philip C. Spector ....Order No. A56140

SAS® System for Mixed Models
by Ramon C. Littell, George A. Milliken, Walter W. Stroup, and
Russell W. Wolfinger ....Order No. A55235

SAS® System for Regression, Second Edition
by Rudolf J. Freund
and Ramon C. Littell.................Order No. A56141

SAS® System for Statistical Graphics, First Edition
by Michael Friendly ....Order No. A56143

SAS® Today! A Year of Terrific Tips
by Helen Carey
and Ginger Carey ....Order No. A55662

The SAS® Workbook and Solutions
(books in this set also sold separately)
by Ron Cody ....Order No. A55594

Statistical Quality Control Using the SAS® System
by Dennis W. King, Ph.D.................Order No. A55232

A Step-by-Step Approach to Using the SAS® System for Univariate
and Multivariate Statistics
by Larry Hatcher
and Edward Stepanski ....Order No. A55072

Survival Analysis Using the SAS® System:
A Practical Guide
by Paul D. Allison ....Order No. A55233

Table-Driven Strategies for Rapid SAS® Applications Development
by Tanya Kolosova
and Samuel Berestizhevsky ....Order No. A55198

Tuning SAS® Applications in the MVS Environment
by Michael A. Raithel ....Order No. A55231

Univariate and Multivariate General Linear Models: Theory and
Applications Using SAS® Software
by Neil H. Timm
and Tammy A. Mieczkowski ....Order No. A55809

Working with the SAS® System
by Erik W. Tilanus ....Order No. A55190

Audio Tapes

100 Essential SAS® Software Concepts (set of two)
by Rick Aster ....Order No. A55309

A Look at SAS® Files (set of two)
by Rick Aster ....Order No. A55207

Frank M. Andrews, Ph.D.

At the time of his death in 1992, Frank was a Research Scientist at the Institute for Social Research, Professor of Psychology, and Professor of Population Planning and International Health, at the University of Michigan. He received the University's Distinguished Research Scientist Award in 1990.

Laura Klem

Senior Social Science Research Associate at the Institute for Social Research and Lecturer in Psychology at the University of Michigan. She teaches and consults on topics of data analysis.

Patrick M. O'Malley, Ph.D.

Senior Research Scientist at the University of Michigan. He has published extensively on the epidemiology and etiology of use and abuse of psychoactive drugs, including the policy implications of the research.

Willard L. Rodgers, Ph.D.

Senior Research Scientist at the Institutite for Social Research and Adjunct Professor in the Sociology Department at the University of Michigan and in the Joint Program in Survey Methodology at the University of Maryland. He teaches courses on the analysis of survey data and the analysis of complex survey data.

Kathleen B. Welch

Statistical Software Consultant at the University of Michigan. She has over 10 years experience using SAS software and has developed and continues to teach several SAS software courses along with providing SAS technical support for the University.

Terrence N. Davidson, Ph.D.

Served on the University of Michigan faculty for twenty years. In the mid-1980's he shifted his career into the K-12 public school sector conducting a variety of research and project activities.

Take the work out of selecting a statistical technique for social science data! This guide addresses social scientists, data analysts, and graduate students who have some knowledge of social science statistics and who want a systematic, highly condensed overview of many of the statistical techniques in current use and the purposes for which each is intended.

A vast array of statistical techniques is provided in an easy-to-use, decision tree approach for you to select and apply to a particular analysis. The most up-to-date statistical and analytical developments are included along with a summary of how each of the techniques is provided through SAS software.

ISBN 1-58025-118-8